Exhibit Design 3

Exhibit Design 3

PBC INTERNATIONAL, INC.

DISTRIBUTOR TO THE BOOK TRADE IN THE UNITED STATES:

Rizzoli International Publications, Inc.
597 Fifth Avenue
New York, NY 10017

DISTRIBUTOR TO THE ART TRADE IN THE UNITED STATES:

Letraset USA
40 Eisenhower Drive
Paramus, NJ 07653

DISTRIBUTOR IN CANADA:

Letraset Canada Limited
555 Alden Road
Markham, Ontario L3R 3L5, Canada

DISTRIBUTED THROUGHOUT THE REST OF THE WORLD BY:

Staff

Executive Director	Penny Sibal-Samonte
Creative Director	Richard Liu
Project Editor	Peter J. Venezia
Production Manager	Kevin Clark
Artists	Donna O'Hare-Patterson
	Kim McCormick
Financial Director	Pamela McCormick

Contents

Foreword 8

Introduction 10

CHAPTER 1 14
Techniques of the Experts

CHAPTER 2 32
Small Exhibits

CHAPTER 3 58
Medium Exhibits

CHAPTER 4 82
Large Exhibits

CHAPTER 5 112
Giant Exhibits

CHAPTER 6 146
Special Areas

CHAPTER 7 176
Multi-Level

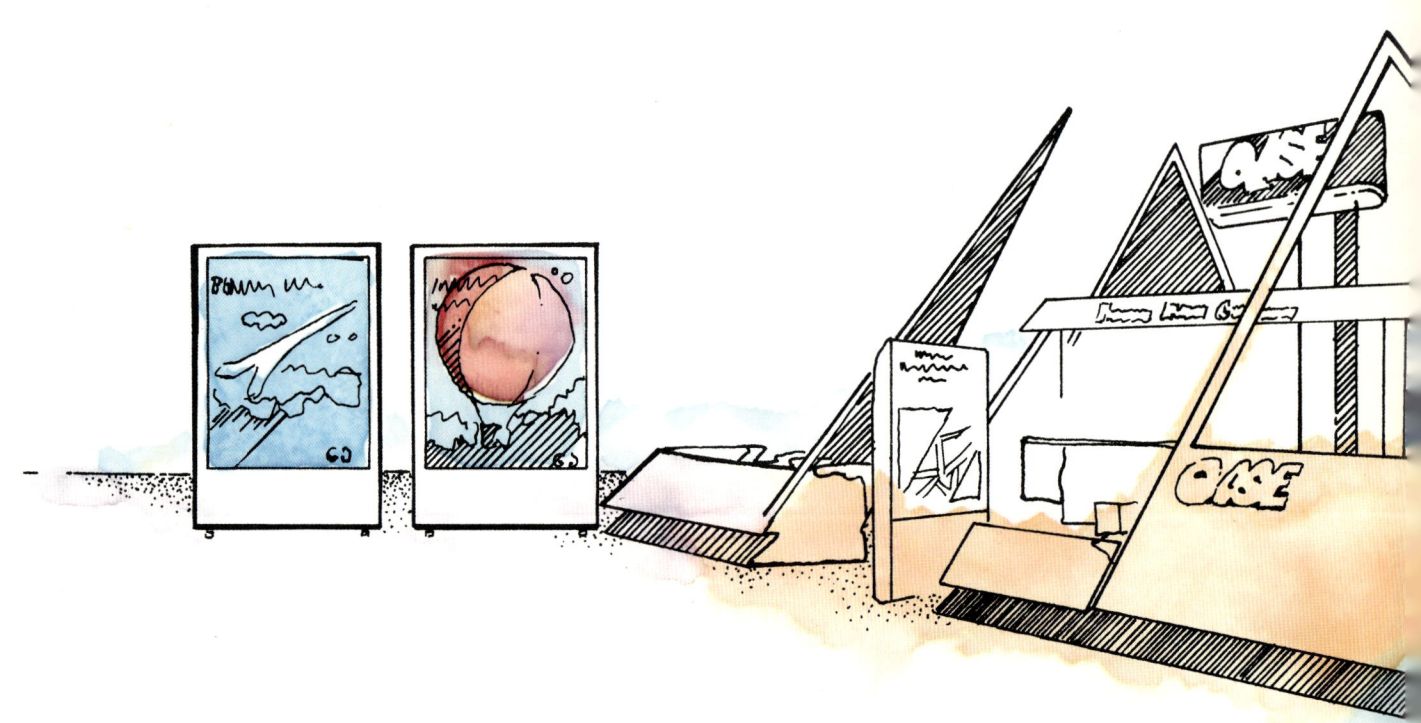

CHAPTER 8   198
Showrooms and Offices

CHAPTER 9   210
Museums

CHAPTER 10   234
Some Interesting Ideas

Index

Foreword

Dan Hartwig
Exhibit Designers & Producers Association

This is the third in a distinguished series of volumes, produced by Bob Konikow, illustrating design and graphics. There has been much written about the philosophy of design, the importance of objectives, and the filling of the clients' needs. Many of the examples shown here achieve some lofty goals and a few might even be considered works of art.

For necessity and clarity, nearly all of these photos document each exhibit without the important element of *people*. Yet, the real function of all exhibits is to attract an audience and to boost sales. Trade shows are a sales environment, and unless exhibits perform that important function—*marketing*—they might end up as an esthetic anachronism.

This book is important to our industry because it "freezes" for us an excellent cross-section of the state of the art. Time pressures, the hustle and bustle and the furor of a show opening are missing. If architecture is indeed "frozen music," then perhaps exhibits without people might be called "frozen marketing."

I hope that these examples are not looked on as just products, but as the culmination of intensive creative effort and skills. W.A. Foster put it aptly: "Quality is never an accident. It is always the result of high intention, sincere effort, intelligent direction, and skillful execution. It represents the wise choice of many alternatives, the cumulative experience of many masters of craftsmanship."

Dan Hartwig
Exhibit Designers & Producers Association

Introduction

Going through the hundreds of entries that came to me during the process of putting together this book has been a fascinating experience, and I'd like to thank all those who helped make this experience possible. Making the final selection was not an easy task, because there are no simple criteria for measuring design creativity or design excellence. It is a matter of personal judgment, tempered by the desire to produce a variety of techniques and approaches in order to make the book more interesting and more useful to its readers.

Some interesting designs unfortunately had to be omitted because of the poor quality of the photographs. We realize how difficult it is to get good photos of exhibits, especially large ones, but there is certainly no excuse for photos that are fuzzy and out of focus. Other photos are difficult to interpret and difficult to discern the exhibits they depict, because of confusing backgrounds, and especially those which are viewed through the center of the subject exhibit. Outlining can occasionally enhance such photos, but not always.

So here is the third collection of contemporary exhibit design, primarily for trade shows, but with some examples of exhibit builders' work in museums and show rooms. The captions are based largely on the descriptions given on the entry blanks, but with some interpretation by the author. The credits, however, have been taken directly from the entries.

We would be very much interested in comments on this year's selection, on suggestions for future books in this series, and especially in description on how readers are using this book.

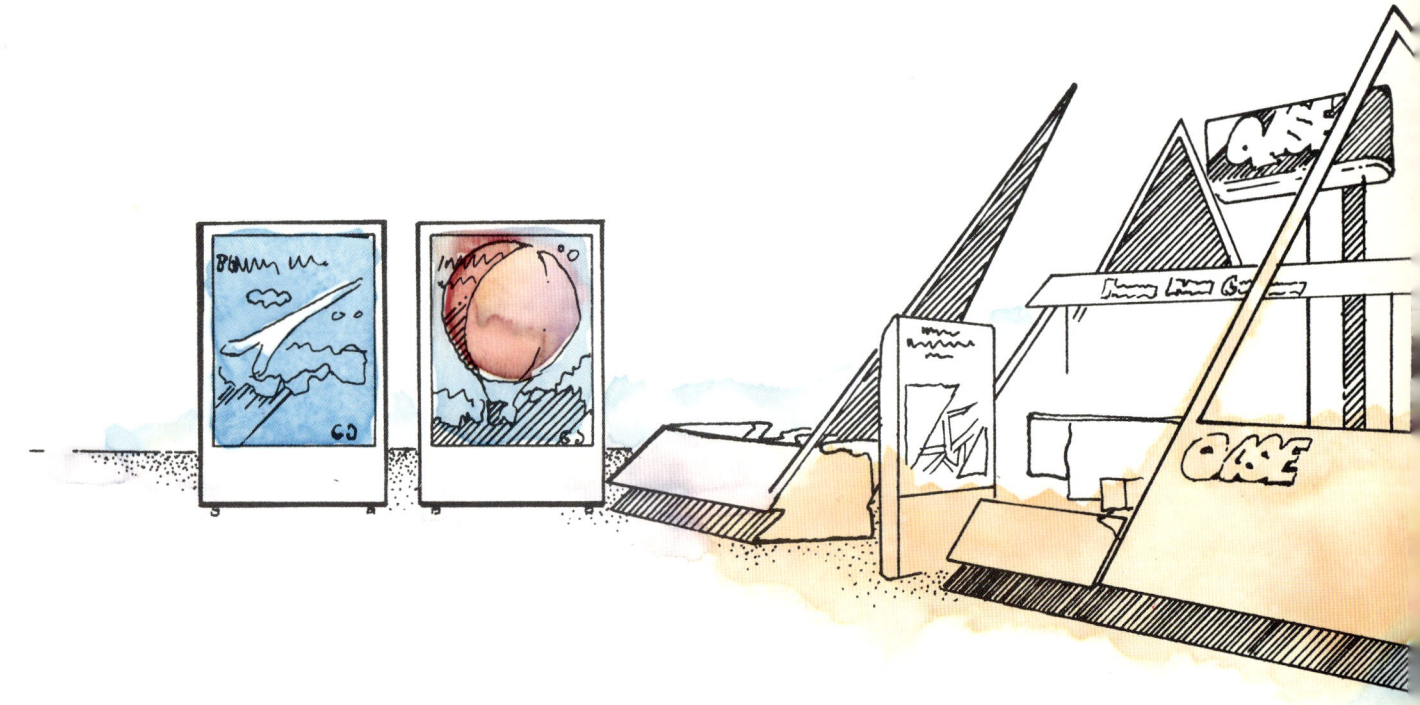

TECHNIQUES OF THE EXPERTS 13

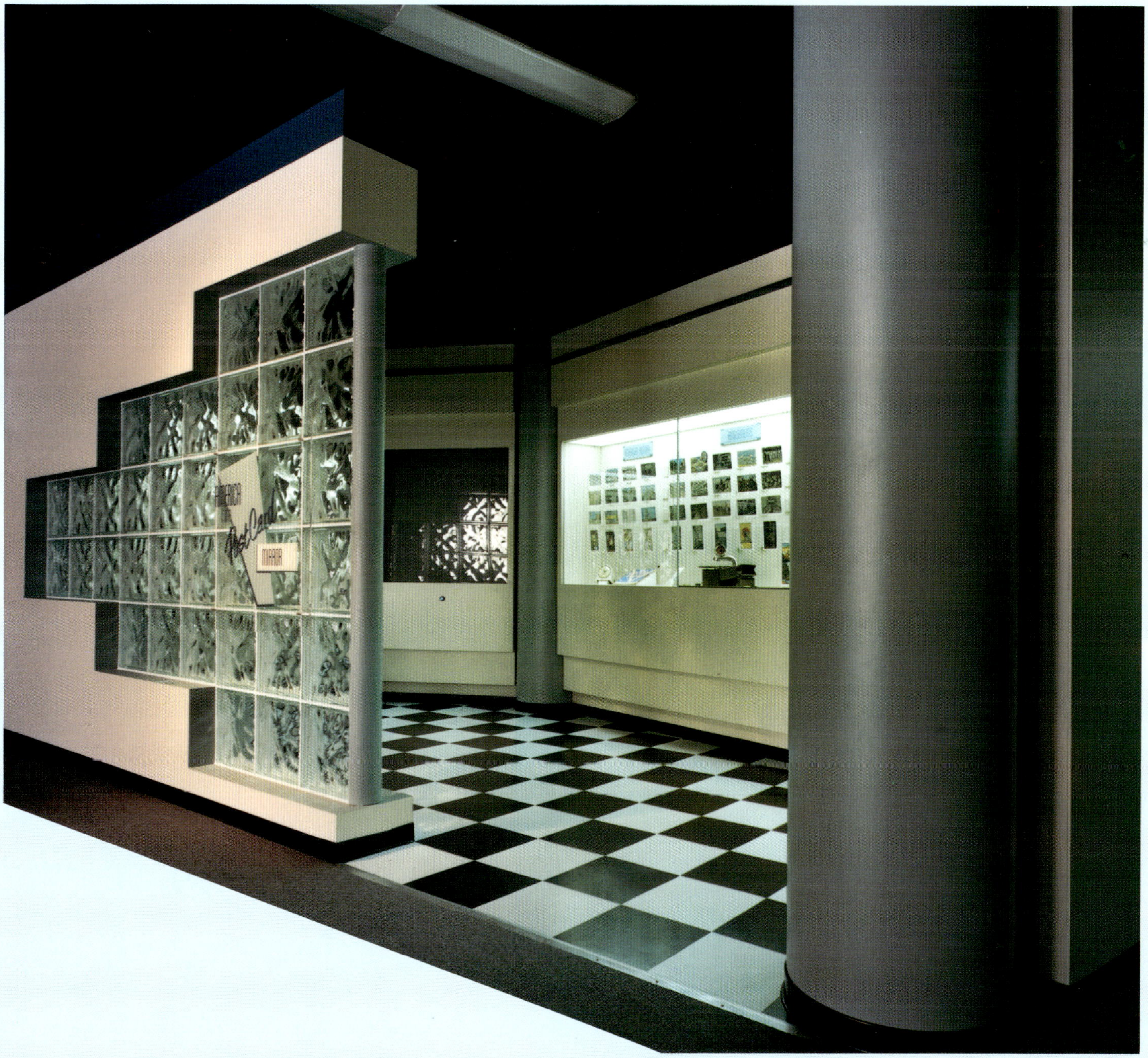

CHAPTER 1
Techniques of the Experts

Mr. Buck, president of Presentation South, Orlando, FL, has both a BA and an MA from Rollins College. Prior to forming his present company, he was supervisor of presentations for the Martin Narietta Corp. His company works in both the commercial exhibit field as well as in museums, and is heavily involved in demonstration techniques.

FUNCTION AND FUN

by Robert L. Buck

Years ago, it was enough to give away a ballpoint pen with your company imprint or to have a drawing for a 16-inch television set, if you wanted to draw a crowd to your trade show booth. Today's exhibitor, however, is looking for qualified leads on a floor where hundreds of other exhibitors are spending millions of dollars to stop and hold the same customers.

Thus, the big question is how to stop and hold the qualified prospect, and how to make him remember your exhibit presentation. To answer this question, we must determine why the serious buyer is there in the first place.

He is there to learn as much about new products and services as he can, in the shortest possible period of time. The competition for his time is so great that he does not wish to work for the information or to pry it out of a poorly designed and manned exhibit. He expects this information to be presented in a simple and easy-to-understand format.

Studies show that operation product exhibits have the highest visitor recall. Believability is high when you can actually put hands on a product and see it work. We all know that people would rather see a product in action rather than read copy or see photos of the items or services offered. Those exhibitors, lucky enough to be able to demonstrate actual products on the trade show floor have an automatic advantage.

But what about the exhibitor who cannot bring his product or service to the trade show floor? It may be too large to fit in a booth, or it simply may not be the type of thing that can be made portable. What about the product that needs a large amount of support equipment to function? What about the "Black Box" type of product that seems to do nothing unless it is inserted into a massive computer system? What about the product that does not show on-the-spot results, such as a drug or a chemical?

In all of these cases, we need a little help to show the product or service in use, as well as its favorable end result. It is here that you can rely on some form of dynamic demonstration device. Though most exhibitors have seen and have operated devices of this kind at EPCOT and science museums, they tend to shy away from them on the exhibit floor, and for several good reasons. Demonstration gear is notoriously prone to damage in shipping. There is usually too little time to shake down the equipment to assure absolute reliability. This equipment is expensive, and even if everything else works out all right, a good demonstration device can become too popular, causing congestion in a booth and bringing in the wrong people.

So what is the answer to the need for dynamically showing off your product or service when you can't actually present it? It is the proper balance of *function* and *fun*.

To make a demonstration device work as a marketing tool, the function must come before the fun. To illustrate, I was at a recent trade show where a friend came up to me and said, "You have to see that magician down at the end of the aisle. He has the wildest contraption that does the goofiest things." When I asked him whose booth it was in, he replied, "I don't know. It's at the end of the aisle. You can't miss it." This was a case of lots of fun but no function. He had watched the show and even participated in it, but had not remembered the product, the name of the company, or anything else about the exhibit.

In addressing the function we must list our exhibit requirements. A demonstration must show the product to its best advantage, it must be short and to the point. It must give the visitor a reason to ask for more information and a follow-up visit. It must isolate the aisle walker from the serious propsect. It must provide qualified leads because that is what the trade show exhibit is all about.

And in accomplishing all of the above, it must be simple to operate, reliable, and safe to travel with.

On the *other* side, you must consider your show audience. The demonstration must be interesting to view passively as well as being interesting to participate in. If the demonstration gear is designed to be operated by a visitor, it should also entertain those watching it being operated. During crowded periods, you do not want potential customers to walk away because of a long line in front of a one-to-one demonstration. This is equally true of actual product demonstrations.

Now you can add fun to the function–not the other way round. Think of fun as taking many forms. The form we are addressing here is one of enjoyment in the intersting way the exhibitor had devised to present his product or service. It does not have to provide belly laughs, but it should provide the visitor with a smile of satisfaction over the fact that his time was not wasted. Remember, it can be just as much fun to discover a way of saving 30 percent on your production costs, as it is to hear a clever "zing" at one of the industry's foibles. Conversely, you don't want the visitor to become bored and walk away before he finds out about that 30 percent savings!

So how do we accomplish this within the exhibit? Once again, it depends on your audience, the size of your booth, and your product or service. Some exhibitors use professionals as demonstrators. Others rely on their own professional or sales staff. The latter need more help.

If we are to follow our rule of carefully developing function prior to fun, we are obviously into a process that will take more than four weeks on the production schedule. Though there are exceptions, a good piece of demonstration gear will take several weeks to design, several weeks to build, and a couple of additional weeks to shake down and establish reliability. Electronic, fiber optics, and other audio-visual devices take time to design and develop. Reliability is the keynote. The visitor to an exhibit will question the end product when he sees that the company can't even get a simple demonstration to work right.

The simpler the demonstration, the easier it is to understand and to operate. A while back, we were asked to demonstrate high-speed valves and pistons, and the fittings that went with them. We controlled air with the valves, with the released air operating pistons which, in turn, struck the bars of a glockenspiel (an early relative of a xylophone). Not only could the visitor see the rapid operation of the pistons, but could hear its effects as well. In addition, the use of industrial equipment to play a tinkly tune on a bell-like instrument had its incongruous and amusing aspects.

What is reasonable for one product does not necessarily work for another. It made great sense for us to use two audio animated parrots, one yellow and one red, to talk about red and yellow pigments at a paint show. The birds made a highly technical story palatable and the audience had fun watching them while they absorbed the information. Using a similar parrot demonstrating a business machine is fun, but it has absolutely nothing to do with the product.

Several years ago, one of our aerospace customers introduced a cellular phone system for military application. Its story was explained by its salesmen, using a presentation on overhead transparency projector. We picked up this tool and used it in the exhibit booth, except that the projector was used by a sketch artist, whose work in process was projected on a large screen. The cells were preprinted with an outline of the phone, and the artists added the visitor's features, so the completed sketch showed him talking on the phone. The prospect brought home a picture of himself using the product, and it cost our client less than a dollar each. The visitor remembered the phone and the presentation, so that the follow-up presentation by a salesman was much more acceptable.

At the other end of the scale, a complex demonstrator may be required to simplify a very complex story. Probably the most complex demonstrator of communications networks is a large fiber optics unit at EPCOT, built for AT&T by Fiber Optics System. It works because it is spectacular, impressive, clear and simple in its presentation. Unfortunately, it is not practical to take this room-size demonstrator to a trade show. But with a change of emphasis from operation to benefits, a smaller, more portable fiber optic display has worked very well for us. We even made one into a game where an unlimited number of people could participate in trying to achieve the system goal. Do not try to tell *everything* about your products or services. Just give the customer enough benefit information, the basics on your product or services, and enough fun to keep the story moving.

Remember function and fun. The function is to demontrate your product and to obtain qualified leads. The fun makes the visitor want to watch your demonstration and to go away with a positive feeling toward your product and your company. Couple these two elements with reliability and ease of presentation, and you will have a successful floor demonstration, in spite of the fact that you had to leave the product itself at home.

Probably one of the best known demonstrations is Sheri's pitch for Racal Milgo at computer shows. The company makes muxes and modems (black boxes) for the computer trade. The end product is not interesting to look at. Its capabilities, on the other hand, are very interesting in that they are system enhancers and money savers.

Sheri's presentation is unique in that she puts down her company's products. She always comes up with her own way of doing things. She demonstrates through the use of complex contraptions that are intended to replace Racal Milgo's tried-and-true equipment. Her substitute equipment always fails with a bang, a crash, smoke, and so on, and she always finishes up her pitch with "I guess you will have to use Racal Milgo's equipment for another year, but I'll be back . . ." During her demonstration, she inserts a lot of complex technical information as she develops her humorous substitutes. Thus, she has effectively sugar-coated a lot of otherwise dry technical data.

The ultimate demonstration, of course, is working hardware, but even here, some creativity can be used. I called on a spring manufacturer a few years ago, and he showed me his spring-making machines, all very large and all state-of-the-art. Wire went in one end and packaged springs came out the other. The equipment was obviously too large to take to a show, and since it was not very dynamic, it would have shown nothing. On the other hand, an array of all his different types of springs was attractive, but did not catch your eye.

I noticed an old cast-iron machine gathering dust in a corner of the plant. When I asked, I was informed that it was used only during peak production periods. It was turned on, and it whirred, clanked, and popped springs out of one end. To me it said "Springs." To the customer it said "Old fashioned." We used it as an aisle stopper, dressed it up and let it spurt out springs during the show. There was no doubt left that this company was manufacturing springs. The company ended up with more orders than it could handle and had to expand its operation after this single show.

To sum up, if you can take it with you and demonstrate it, do it. If not, try to come up with a method of demonstration that will make your points and leave your visitor with a memory of your fine products and services. Remember fun *and* function!

Ralph Holker, president of Holker & Barry Inc., Brooklyn, NY approaches his projects with the eye of a designer, which is not strange, since his training and his original entry to the industry was as a designer. But as he points out here, the objective of an exhibit is not esthetic but practical. A good design must not only look good, but must also help meet the exhibitor's objectives. This piece is an updated revision of one which he originally wrote for *Medical Exhibits & Promotion* several years ago.

EXHIBIT EVALUATION: A NEW APPROACH

by Ralph L. Holker

The major problem inherent in the criticism of contemporary exhibit design is that exhibits do not have an identity of their own. Outside the exhibit industry, there is little known about the field of commercial exhibits. As a result, exhibit design has been approached as a combination of architecture, corporate image and industrial "show-biz."

Why is this? Exhibit design has not been taught as a separate discipline. Designers have drawn from their backgrounds in architecture, interiors, advertising, and industrial design to solve exhibit problems. The real purpose of exhibits has not been sufficiently defined for designers to apply their expertise in solving specific problems. With no esthetic criteria, one exhibit design can be as valid as another. To set in a new direction, we must examine the reasons for this lack of identity, define various types of exhibits, and set criteria for evaluation of exhibits.

Why this lack of identity? Basically, the reason is that few people recognize the magnitude of exhibits and trade show participation today. I would venture to state that even exhibit designers have little idea of how many other designers share their problems and frustrations. Few realize that every week, in every major city, at least one meeting and trade show is taking place where exhibits are the background for transmitting information to everyone from pickle packers to brain surgeons.

Relatively few people see any one exhibit. Due to their short life span and diverse geographical locations, exhibits are seen only by those who attend trade shows and medical meetings. The exhibits are seldom seen "in the flesh" by their designers. As a result, exhibit designers have the least opportunity of all those working in the major design disciplines to examine their designs, or the designs of others, in a crowded exhibit hall. Until fairly recently, if exhibits were seen at all, they were seen as small black-and-white photos in marketing trade publications. The photographs showed only one part of the complex interrelationship between three-dimensional design, two-dimensional design, product presentation, and the sales staff interaction with buyers. In addition, the copy usually pointed out how unimportant the design was to the success of the exhibit.

Designers usually drift into exhibit design and draw on their experiences in other graphic and three-dimensional design disciplines. There has been little dialog among those who have chosen exhibit design as their major discipline. Without a platform for the exchange of ideas, exhibit designers are isolated from opportunities to engage in meaningful dialog. There is not enough contact between exhibit designers and design educators. This is reflected in student portfolios that are too often filled with projects that redesign successful pieces of furniture, create pretentious graphics, or solve esoteric human engineering problems, but seldom present designs for exhibits. Because commercial exhibits have not been "successfully" designed by "name" designers, they do not seem to be suitable projects for undergraduate study. Exhibits have generally been evaluated by grouping them according to economic considerations or memory value with total indifference to their function. An obvious error in categorizing exhibits by memory value (for esthetic evaluation) is that there is a tendency to judge exhibits by size rather than design.

The fact that exhibits have very different purposes has been overlooked. An exhibit in an "order-writing" type of show has such different objectives from one that is primarily directed to giving information, that they cannot possibly be compared. An exhibit that is used one time, to communicate one message to a select group of buyers, cannot be compared to one which is designed to change its face with each change of audience. What is needed, then, is some logical separation of general categories of exhibit design.

To begin with, exhibits should be divided into two major groups, each with distinct characteristics. In the first group are exhibits that communicate a single message —the characteristics of a product or group of related products to a homogeneous audience. In the second category, are multiple message exhibits. The exhibit structure is readily adaptable to communicate messages about a wide variety of products to a diverse group of observers. Obviously, these two basic categories can be further subdivided and defined in greater detail. By examining the fundamental requirements of these two groups, we can see that each must be approached in a different way, much the way the design of a race car or family sedan must be approached differently, although both are automobiles.

Multiple Message Exhibits

The majority of exhibits designed today are multiple message exhibits. This is primarily a stage, a mini-environment, which is compatible with a variety of graphic additions. It plays to one audience today and another a week or a month from now. Each audience is interested in different information.

The fact that there are so many multiple message exhibits and that many are so poorly designed is one reason why exhibit design is held in low esteem by professional designers. ("If I have to design that kind of junk, I don't want any part of it!") The criteria for evaluation of this type of exhibit must be a combination of several factors, some technical, some visual. An esthetic evaluation must first determine if the dominating structure enhances or detracts from its basic function—to communicate a message.

Are the materials used for construction of multiple exhibits suitable for multiple setup and dismantling and shipping back and forth across the country? Does the designer consider the materials to be relative to that function? Today, the answer to these technical questions is an overwhelming NO. The primary structural components of lacquered particle board are poor imitations of interiors. They are heavy to handle, costly to ship, and extremely prone to damage. The fragility of the exhibit components requires heavy shipping shells or special handling in padded furniture vans. New materials—plastics, for example—that are less fragile and lighter in weight, are available and being used by designers to reduce refurbishing, transportation and drayage costs. The use of these materials is good engineering, but does not automatically create good design. Does the contemporary designer use these new materials in imaginative ways that take advantage of their organic design possibilities, or have they been used to "round out" the traditional structures? New materials in exhibits, as with new materials throughout history, have always imitated the materials they replaced.

In determining criteria for evaluation, we must also take into consideration how the graphics are presented. Are they visually integrated as part of the structure? Can they easily be changed? Are the products displayed effectively or do they look like an afterthought?

One final consideration in design evaluation important to good multi-message exhibit design is ease of assembly and dismantling. The amount of money used in this often costly process comes out of the total budget. The larger the amount of the budget spent on services, the smaller the amount available to communicate the message.

Single Message Exhibits

The single message exhibit is a rare design opportunity. Its purpose as a marketing tool can be narrowly defined. It portrays a limited message to a limited group of observers. Since it may be used only once and then discarded, the fragility of the components is of minimal consideration. In fact, components that are easily discarded may have a cost advantage over more durable materials.

Unfortunately, single message exhibits are generally also "structure exhibits." Whether small or large, they are overwhelming imitative in structure, aping architecture and using 50-year-old architectural criteria for esthetic evaluation. They communicate on a two-dimensional level, at best with bas relief signs, slide presentations or silk-screened typography. Remove the signs and products from one exhibit and install them in one of equal opulence and few people would know the difference. The structures of most single message exhibits have little or nothing to do with the messages they are supposed to communicate.

Consequently, the exhibits of architecturally-oriented designers tend to emphasize structure over message and the graphics become billboards that ignore the third dimension. Viewing exhibits as architecture has created superficial criteria for evaluation. The walnut paneling simulating the president's office of yesteryear is disdained by the contemporary designer, while imitative curtained wall structures are praised since they look

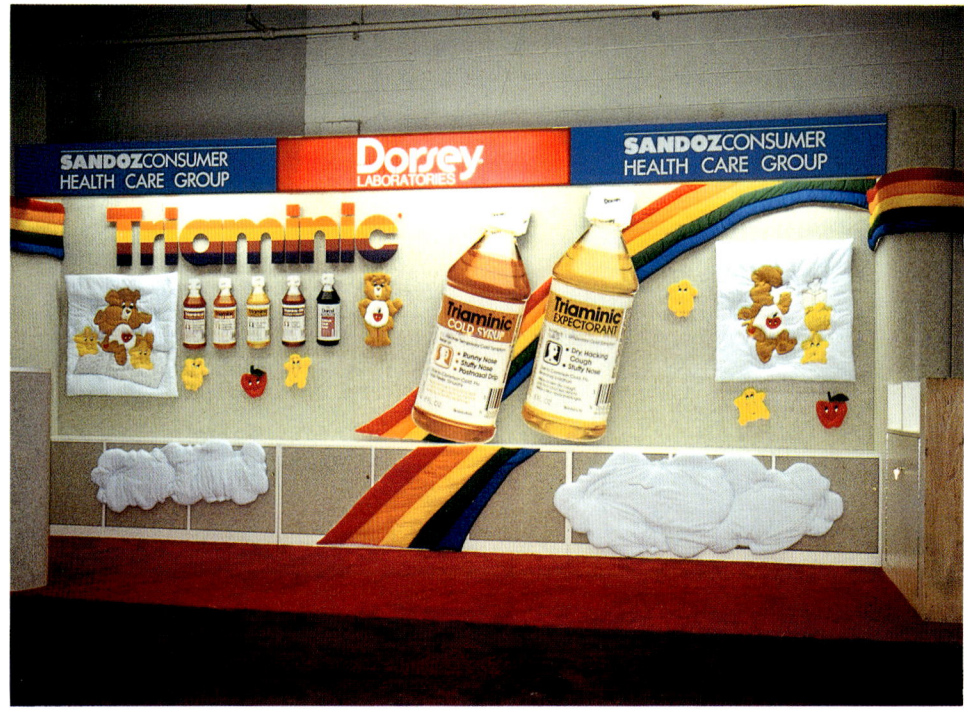

expensive. The structure, in such cases, only communicates a subliminal message of the overall corporate image.

The structure should be evaluated on how well it functions as a three-dimensional graphic selling environment. Webster's definintion of graphic is "to describe clearly and vividly." This is the function of an exhibit—to describe clearly and vividly the economy, usefulness and/or superiority of something. It should be a criterion for evaluating single message exhibits.

The structure of a single message exhibit must reinforce the graphic message. An inflated mushroom might be more valid than tinted plexiglass and brushed aluminum. A structure designed to keep out all but 10 or 15 percent of the total attendance might be more valid than an elaborate presentation that entertains 85–90 percent of the non-decision-makers, but is staged in what is now considered a "contemporary structure." An exhibit that can be thrown away might be more valid, than one that costs $25 per man hour to dismantle and pack.

In order to comprehensively evaluate the totality of the exhibiting process, we must know more than just how the structure looks. What is its purpose and how does it relate to other information-producing stimuli? What information is the exhibit expected to deliver? What information is the booth personnel expected to deliver? What information is the brochure expected to deliver? The answers to these questions will supply the data necessary to evaluate the graphic exhibit as a valid medium of communication.

Does the combination of structure, graphics, products, and booth personnel have a visual impact that sets it apart from rows and rows of similar structures? The evaluation must recognize that each exhibitor has his own unique objectives and should be judged on how well the designer has creatively transferred these objectives to a graphic, three-dimensional, living, sales tool. The result will be better use of each exhibit dollar and a lower cost in effectively communicating.

How can all this be accomplished? Certainly this book and its predecessors, "Exhibit Design" and "Exhibit Design 2," fill a long neglected need. A next step might be to sponsor a photo essay contest to find new ways to see exhibits through photography. The multiple photograph essays will give designers the opportunity to see not only an overall view, but also close-ups of sales reps, buyers, graphics presentations, and imaginative construction methods. In addition, a research library should be established. Models and photographs of outstanding esthetic solutions to design problems would be displayed. The presentation models would give designers an excellent opportunity to study the works of their contemporaries and see those works as the three-dimensional structures that they are. Accompanying texts could explain the design rationale. Exhibit designers need to become more articulate in developing and presenting design theories. And most importantly, a system must be implemented to maintain a continuing dialog among designers, educators, students, and critics.

The Smallest Exhibit Size Can Seem Like the Biggest Headache

by Scott Gray

Mr. Gray, formerly director of Communications for the International Exhibitors Association, currently heads his own public relations/writing organization Whole Night Media, in the Washington area. This essay is adapted from a series of articles that originally appeared in *Tradeshow Week*, of which he is a Contributing Editor.

They are the most common size of exhibits in tradeshows: the "ten-footer," usually 10′ × 10′ or 8′ × 10′, and for many exhibitors they represent the biggest challenge. They don't offer much room for showing equipment, which makes product presentations difficult and often impossible. Also, they can get lost in forests of multiple-story exhibits, islands, and peninsulas.

But they are also often the only size exhibit a small company can afford. And portable exhibits and systems make the ten-footer an even more affordable venture, although custom-designed ten-foot exhibits will probably give a more distinctive image to the company. John Sturm, president, Contempo Design, said the difference in impact between a 10-footer and a 20-footer are worlds apart. But 10-footers are not doomed to failure just because of their diminutive size. In fact, foot for foot, a small exhibit can be as effective in the right show as a larger booth, if the exhibit manager follows the right steps, according to Sturm.

Preshow

All exhibits, large or small, must have at least one objective for the show and a set of measurable goals to support the objective. Consider the unique possibilities of the small booth when setting objectives. For example, while demonstrating a large piece of equipment is out of the question, a 10-footer gives you the opportunity to showcase particular selling points in a more intimate setting.

Design and construction must begin months in advance. It is no simple matter for an exhibit designer/producer to build a 10′ custom exhibit. Even putting an exhibit together from a system or purchasing a portable takes time in developing proper graphics.

When planning the design, consider the additional uses the exhibit will have. Will it become part of a larger, expanded exhibit at some point? Or will this be a one-time use?

Be sure the company's identification is easily identifiable on the exhibit. With a small booth, you don't have any room to be subtle. But don't put too much copy onto the exhibit, Sturm warns, or it will get lost. The entire exhibit will get lost if you don't provide adequate lighting.

Remember that openness is crucial to the 10′ exhibit. If you leave the side rails up, and put a table in front of the exhibit, you have effectively built a cell which encloses your staff and keeps attendees out. Make sure the design opens up the exhibit, especially on the aisle.

- Preshow promotion is critical if you are going into a large show, especially one that is national in scope. The big exhibits will naturally draw the attendees, since they generally have the prime exhibit spaces, and the 10-footers are stashed somewhere back along the wall. Since a 10′ exhibitor's budget is probably limited, the promotion may also be limited. But this is not necessarily a problem, because for very little money, exhibitors can design and print their own guides to purchasing the type of equipment they are showing. Also, similar publications might be available from trade magazines which exhibitors can overprint with their names and logos.

- It is important for the smaller exhibitor, especially one using the show's official service contractor, to get all forms in on time and to complete them fully in virtually every instance. If the form is completed well in advance and all information is provided, the labor and equipment will be there on time. However, it is especially important for the exhibit manager to check in at the service desk upon arrival to make sure all is in order.

- In large and small companies alike, it is critical that the employees, especially those who will be staffing the exhibit, understand the importance of the booth to the company. Often 10-footers are used to represent a company in a regional or dealer show, and the corporate exhibit manager is not on site to ensure professionalism. If the representatives of the show believe that the exhibit showcases the company, the booth's effectiveness will be improved and lead follow-up will be easier.

At the Show

- There is a twist to training booth personnel for the smaller booth. Rather than getting the attendees qualified and into the booth, the exhibitor must get the attendee qualified and OUT of the booth. There simply is not enough room for sales staff to give a full product presentation within the confines of a 10′ exhibit. Sturm noted that a major mistake exhibitors make when planning a 10′ × 10′ is to try to include a seating area. That is not to say that you don't spend all the time a prospect wants to discuss your product, but remember the unquantified, but very real, "clog factor": the number of attendees passing up your exhibit rises in direct proportion to the number clogging access to it.

- Since a very valid short-term goal of the exhibit may be simply to have a presence and gather names of prospects—and not to make sales at the show—the lead gathering system is very important. There isn't space to sit down and take an order, but there is space to get a credit card type registration system imprint. The follow-up of these leads is more important to the company which has not written any sales at the show because they represent the entire take from the show. If the exhibit is to show any return on investment, it will be as a direct result of those leads.

© 1987 by Tradeshow Week, Inc, Los Angeles, CA (213) 826-5696

After the Show
Follow-up, follow-up, follow-up.

Even exhibitors with the smallest booths must evaluate the effectiveness of the effort. This includes a thorough evaluation of the goals and whether they were met and what the return on investment was. But a good evaluation does not have to be complex. An exhibitor does not even need a computer to conduct a professional evaluation. Answering several key questions will provide a good evaluation:

- Did you meet your objective(s)?
- Did you fulfill your goals?
- How many people did your exhibit staff talk to?
- How many of the key prospects that you invited visited your exhibit?
- What were all of your exhibit costs?
- What were all your sales at the show?
- What are your potential sales after the show?
- Was the exhibit cost-effective?
- Should you be in this show next year?

The corporate exhibit manager may find that getting sales staff to provide such information, especially when the exhibit is used in a regional or dealer show, is like pulling teeth. This is where the team-building which should have taken place early on is important.

The effectiveness of an exhibit is not necessarily related to its size. Careful planning and follow through allows the exhibitor to utilize 10′ exhibiting to the company's advantage.

Exhibit Design that Uses Systems

by Don J. Lyon

Mr. Lyon has had long experience with the design and development of systems for trade show exhibits. Currently, he is associated with Octanora Ltd.

Like so many projects, the page on this one is blank, the show date set in stone, and the particulars grind within your mind: multiple booth configurations; varying height restrictions; different products, each with different graphics, to be featured; demands for lower shipping and installation costs.

These are just some of the challenges facing exhibit designers, not to mention demanding budgetary limitations, production capabilities, and turn-around time. The complexity of exhibit design has come a long way since a painted sign hung from the back wall was considered "state of the art."

Today's exhibit manager can no longer use a single exhibit for all the shows on his schedule, but must acquire a variety of presentation packages for a multitude of corporate objectives. He searches for new approaches to fit within limited budgets which often rule out standard production practices.

The development of architectural products, lightweight extrusions and modular fixturing materials are providing sophisticated exhibit systems which can easily satisfy these new marketing requirements. More than 15 years ago, table top exhibits and 10′ portable displays began to appear on the scene, and ever since then, we've classified any construction material other than wood as a system. More types of systems have been developed and produced since then, permitting a great variety of customer design. The flexible use of materials can inexpensively accomplish sometimes difficult types of construction.

Unfortunately, the assumption has arisen that all systems are essentially the same: labor-intensive, and nothing more than a frame for supporting graphics. This short-sighted approach has denied us the experience of what some systems can do for our custom design and production capabilites. Today's systems, whether they are component or construction based, are lightweight, modular, and consist of pre-engineered components, with standardized measurements, and usually supported by a full line of accessories and finishes.

The biggest problem in understanding systems, their design, application, and economics, is usually the time required to become familiar with them. People thought their lives or their businesses would be better organized by turning on a personal computer, until they saw all the documentation there was to read. Once you're over that hurdle, whether with PCs or with exhibit systems, you will find that, indeed, your business and your life can be improved and simplified.

There are basically three types of exhibit systems on the market today, and each has its role to play:

> *Lightweight/Portable Systems*—designed for ease in transportation and installed by the exhibitor, using no tools. These tend to be produced in 10′ increments and can be combined for larger booth arrangements. Lightweights include framed panels with hooks, connectors, tabs, hinges, poles, expandable frames, disposable units, and table tops. Panels are usually of lightweight material covered in a laminate, Velcro, or vinyl, in a variety of colors.
>
> *Component Systems*—usually of predesigned panels in a variety of sizes and surface finishes, including plexiglass. The various components allow for custom design applications, can be used for large display formats and resemble contemporary wood construction. Some of these systems can be used as portables, but will require standard shipping cases for larger exhibits.
>
> *Construction Systems*—a direct alternative to wood construction. These systems require the skill of an exhibit designer, and a full-service exhibit house for production. The components are engineered with a multitude of design and construction capabilities, pre-finished in a variety of colors, and have a full line of accessories. They usually consist of material from the architectural market, and include aluminum extrusions, antenna trussing, space frames, tubes with clamps, and geodesic domes.

These modular exhibit systems offer some unique design advantages in solving your clients' objectives. In difficult areas of construction, the systems provide connections of various degrees, eliminating the concern of producing and finishing details such as compound angles. Rear-illuminated light boxes, suspended headers, custom counters, backwall panels, kiosks, radius corners or towers can be constructed without heavy wood framing.

Some extrusion and space frame systems provide great free span capabilities for ceiling and canopy treatments that can slope, cantilever, curve, or create eye-catching geometric shapes. Some construction systems also offer customer double-deck materials that surpass standard structural engineering requirements. The newest additions are geodesic domes available in various diameters, sections of which may be used for unique wall or canopy treatments.

Most exhibits built from systems reduce production time, refurbishing, handling, crating, shipping costs, and labor for set up and dismantling. They offer economical solutions to low budget exhibitors or exciting structural achievements for larger projects with flexible requirements that easily expand with a company's growth and marketing goals. The unique characteristic of system-designed displays is that they can be redesigned time and time again, or expanded upon, without scrapping the original structure.

Most quality manufacturers of systems offer training programs, design and construction support services, as well as design and estimating confirmations. Established exhibit systems today have developed all the construction components necessary to complete a tradeshow exhibit design. Though the design capacity varies from one system to another, most have produced everything from panel connectors to high tech lighting, making it unnecessary for you to engineer additional hardware or fittings.

Systems can be easily integrated into wood-constructed exhibits to create a unique visual statement, or to increase the modular capabilities of existing displays. By utilizing systems that are supported by a world-wide network of exhibit builders, you can offer a turnkey design and service package for your clients who exhibit overseas, or provide services for foreign exhibitors here in the United States.

Systems offer the unique opportunity of providing your clients with one of the most advanced tradeshow marketing tools available. Exhibits can be redesigned to meet the marketing objectives as they change from one show to the next. Your client can attend a medical, a financial, an engineering, or a manufacturing show, either national or regional, with a custom-tailored design for each appearance. A designer can rent custom system exhibits according to his client's show itinerary, tailored for the changing market, and shipping no more than products, brochures, and graphics. The net result from reduced shipping, elimination of storage, maintenance, and ownership, is the ability to provide multiple custom system exhibits produced within your client's existing tradeshow budgets.

Systems will enable designers and producers to position their conceptual services into the next generation of exhibit design, where we can treat trade show exhibiting as professional marketing and promotional events. Systems are making this design/marketing evolution possible, and permitting exhibit designers and producers to realize greater compensation for their marketing expertise in the tradeshow exhibit industry.

Mr. Kitzing, president of Kitzing Incorporated, has long been an ardent believer in the marketing function of the trade show exhibit. A designer by background, he was the 1983 winner of the Hazel Hays Award, presented by the Exhibit Designers & Producers Association.

A Machine for Selling In

by Fred Kitzing

The development of architecture during the twentieth century was synchronized with the acceleration and mechanization of society. The concept of architectural beauty evolved from a decorative viewpoint to the mid-century functionalism of Mies van der Rohe and Le Corbusier. A new perception, a new orientation of design replaced what had been. Corbusier pronounced, "A house is a machine for living in."

Trade show exhibits are in a similar evolvement. Mid-century manufacturers, riding a crest of heavy consumer demand and full capacity production, could afford exhibits based on arbitrary esthetic appeal. Trade show managers in the fifties, the era that seems so long ago and with so different a sales environment, gave prizes for the best-looking exhibits.

Times have changed. Competition among manufacturers grew as domestic and foreign markets diminished. Today, sales are the prime need of every manufacturer and every service organization.

Trade shows have emerged from the "convention" status of the fifties to a strong sales-generating position. Today, only direct marketing commands more business promotion investment than the trade show medium, according to figures released by *Business Marketing* in 1987.

Advertising	$8,589,371,000
Direct Marketing	30,850,000,000
Trade Shows	21,000,000,000
Sales Promotion	7,616,900,000
Incentives	15,065,871,000
Public Relations	2,405,300,000
Research	2,190,200,000

Exhibit design is synchronizing with this need for sales. Exhibit design for personal taste is evolving into design for an exhibit structure and sales support material that reaches sales objectives. The exhibit is on its way to becoming a machine for selling.

The exhibit designer, trained in esthetics and construction techniques, now finds himself obligated to a broadened discipline. He has the obligation to become a marketer, a marketer who uses his skills in developing the dynamics of selling on the trade show floor.

In this new orientation, does the exhibit designer discard esthetics? No. He utilizes his esthetics in vitalizing the exhibit's marketing thrust. The exhibit designer engineers the exhibitor's sales tactics. Not always, nor even frequently, are sales closed on the trade show floor. The exhibit designer, with his client, defines objectives for the project, if not for sales on the floor, for leads that can be converted into sales following the show, or sales that result from the projection of a defined image.

With sales objectives, the exhibit designer has a guide that directs his creativity. Sales objectives remove the design from arbitrary decisions based on arbitrary tastes.

The exhibit designer's function, in this period of tough business competition, is making his designs sales-functional. Because the progressive exhibit designer understands trade show dynamics, he investigates the various factors that are part of those dynamics. He integrates those factors:

- the product
- the product's appeal to the prospective audience
- the trade show attendance
- the segment of that attendance that represents the product's market
- characteristics of those prospective buyers
- strategies that will bring those prospective buyers into selling range
- the means by which the exhibit personnel will communicate the product's advantages to the prospective buyer and adjust those advantages to particular needs and wants
- the means of recording performance and results.

Doing this, the exhibit designer becomes an engineer—engineering sales for his exhibiting client.

The exhibit designer also has to develop the mechanical properties of his exhibit design: how to break down the structure into parts that are easily assembled, convenient to pack, with minimum weight and low maintenance, the exhibit designer must present his development in an appealing form, attractive and comprehensible to his client.

Delineation of the development in drawings, renderings or models must appeal to a client audience that is not as visually experienced and visually oriented as a designer.

There are circumstances and situations that inhibit logical development of the functional sales-productive exhibit. In a corporation the setting of objectives and parameters is frequently delegated to a second or third layer of manager. The preliminary decision concerning the implementation of the design is made by a committee that is unaware of the well-organized trade show campaign. Preliminary preferences are then relayed to the top level executive who has had no input, no part in setting objectives, and makes his decisions based on taste preferences.

The successful trade show campaign has strong top management backing and involvement, insightful sales-oriented input from corporate authority, and an interface with the exhibit designer that provides information on which to develop a sales-producing design.

No architect, not even Mies van der Rohe or Le Corbusier, would design a dwelling without input from those who plan to live in it. The interchange, the wants and requirements of the future tenants, known to those tenants, combined with the design possibilities, known to the architect, assures a structure that is both functional and esthetically appealing.

Given adequate information and the opportunity of developing ideas with decision makers, the designer can create a hard-core, sales-function structure with visual appeal. In other words, a machine for selling.

Mr. McDonald is Chairman of the Board of Greyhound Exhibitgroup Inc., the nation's largest designer and producer of trade show exhibits, with ten offices nationwide. Like many top executives in the industry, he entered the field with a design background.

How to Get the Design you Need

By Leo S. McDonald

We all know that design is a major factor in such products as automobiles, furniture, clothing, jewelry, and even homes. It gives an emotional tinge to these products, and we respond to emotion and thus to design. One would think that there is no emotion involved, and therefore little need for design, in the kind of business transaction that goes on in a trade show booth. But there is indeed emotion in even the most technical buying decision. Therefore, design has a part to play.

But exhibit design is not just styling, the sort of styling you expect in jewelry. It must contribute in an emotional sense, but it must also embody such practical aspects as functioning in the complex environment of a trade show. In this sense it is like design in architecture or furniture production; it must be functional as well as esthetically pleasing.

Good exhibit design starts with an esthetic appeal, of course. It must first of all catch the eye of the passerby and arouse his interest. But it must go further than that—it must satisfy the interest it has aroused. It must properly display the informative content of the exhibit, holding the viewer's interest long enough to convey the desired message. It must also be selective, serving to attract that fraction of the show attendance who are real prospects.

How does one achieve good design? It starts with the involvement of the client, the exhibitor. It is not necessary that the client's representative in the exhibit process be a designer. He must primarily understand his company's marketing goals and have the ability to convey these goals to the exhibit designer. He must realize that a design produced without the guidelines of marketing goals may be esthetically pleasing, but cannot be an effective exhibit. He cannot sit back and say, "You're the expert. Come back with some ideas." Good design is achieved by a partnership between the designer and the exhibitor. The former provides the technical input; the latter, the marketing input. The better the team works together, the better the design.

Thus, the first two elements that are important to the success of an exhibit are a knowledgeable client and a creative designer. Two additional elements that are essential are an adequate budget, and a competent builder. And finally, there must be an adequately trained and motivated crew to man the booth.

In order for the corporate exhibit manager to work closely and effectively with teh designer, he must not overwork himself. He must not try to work with half-a-dozen exhibit houses on the same project. When this happens, the effort to put all competitors on an equal basis and to get proposals that can be compared, too often results in specs that are so detailed that they inhibit creativity. The ideal is to work with one house and one designer who knows your approach and can be given

This will give you a list of competent designer/producers, any one of whom should be able to develop a satisfactory solution to your trade show marketing problem. But be sure to give the one you select enough time, for time is often the factor that causes otherwise well-planned projects to run into difficulties. Sometimes there are valid reasons why time is short. Most frequently, the development of a new product, scheduled for introduction at a major show, is slower than expected, and you cannot keep up with your original timetable. Under such circumstances, keep your exhibit house fully informed. If you suspect a delay, let its rep know about it as early as possible, so his designer can take this into account, and can leave an escape route. However, you can take heart from the fact that many great exhibits have been produced very quickly under pressure, but you usually have to pay more for the shortened schedule, and you forfeit the luxury of mid-course corrections and second and improved thoughts.

Getting an effective exhibit designed, built, and installed is indeed a challenging task. But the results are worth the game. you will feel a sense of pride, and a great satisfaction, when you look over the floor, and see that your exhibit is outstanding, that it is functioning well, that it is reaching the objectives you set for it.

But many companies have set up the requirement that competitive bids be obtained on all projects, making it necessary to work with a number of designer/producers. When this is the case, the exhibit manager should select no more than three qualified companies. He should give each of these a set of specifications, and ask for a proposal. But the specifications should not be so detailed that they inhibit imagination. Ask for preliminary designs, so that the designers will have an opportunity to step outside the specs and suggest better or less expensive approaches.

It often happens that one of the three proposals, at the preliminary stage, is obviously superior. In that case, there is no point in wasting the time of either the exhibit manager or of the other two houses. Dismiss the unfortunate two, and continue to develop the outstanding design. If all three have possibilities, continue further with all three companies. Often the best ideas occur in the latter phases of design development.

To obtain the best results from this procedure, it is advisable to agree upon a fee to be paid to the unsuccessful competitors. This is especially true for a large and complicated exhibit. The fee need not be so large that it includes a full profit margin, but by assuring that basic costs will be covered, you can expect a more serious effort to be applied to the problem.

The success of this approach is based on the assumption that each of the exhibit houses that you have invited to compete is competent and creative. You should be willing to work closely with any one of the three. How do you find creative designers and competent builders? The best way, in my opinion, is through referral. Get to know exhibit houses. As you visit trade shows, especially during set-up, make a note of which companies have exhibits you think are well-designed, and find out who produced them. When the show opens, take another look to see if they really work and are well-attended.

Pick out the three leaders in this survey, and get acquainted with them. Pay a visit to their shops; talk to their principals; check out their financial soundness; ask them for the names of additional clients on their current list.

USWEST

Welcome to the U S WEST Technical Exhibition at ISS '87. Inside you will explore actual working demonstrations of U S WEST's current ISDN trials, the most comprehensive ISDN trials in the world.

Talk with the switch manufacturers, terminal equipment vendors, network managers and customers who, with U S WEST, are writing ISDN history.

CHAPTER 2
Small Exhibits

Every exhibit project is a challenge to the designer. But according to most professionals, the design of the small exhibit (400 square feet and under) presents a special challenge.

There are a number of reasons for this, the first of which is fiscal in nature. The smaller spaces are usually taken by smaller companies, with limited resources and less sophistication in the exhibit market place. Their budgets tend to be lower and their expectations higher, and sometimes unrealistic.

Considering these factors, it is a wonder that so many small booths are attractive and eye-catching. The selection shown in this chapter illustrate many of the techniques that today's designers are using to make a noteworthy structure in a space as small as ten foot square.

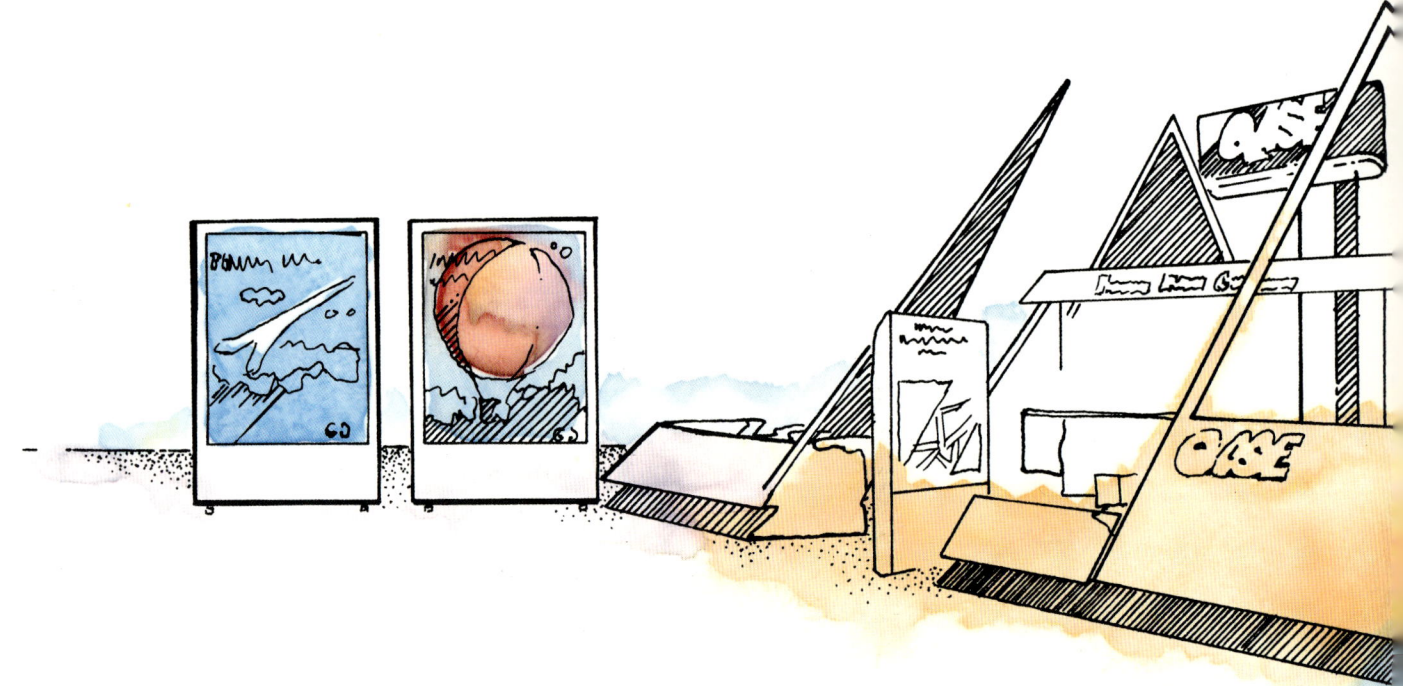

Exhibitor: U S West Direct
Producer: Exhibits Inc.

In order to meet a tight project budget, a stock exhibit system was customized with unique graphics and a custom counter feature which, traveling alone, can also be used as a speaker's podium.

Exhibitor:	Digital Technology Inc./ Interface Technologies
Producer/Designer:	Downing Displays Inc.

Two sister companies are able to share a structure, since each of the seven panels is reversible, with a different loop fabric on each side. The floorstands and shelving are interchangeable.

Exhibitor:	Bell Bagg
Producer:	Heritage Display Group, Dallas
Designer:	Ken Konke

A series of vertical panels, each with its own header and illumination, supplemented by cylindrical pedestals of varying heights, allows for maximum product exposure and portability, all at a modest budget.

Exhibitor:	LeCroy
Producer:	David Brace Displays Inc.
Designers:	Jeanne Fornes, Tom Pafk

With a demand for multiple configurations and a hi-tech look, the designers developed a series of 40-inch modules, each with an internal wall of light that illuminated the titles and the graphic transparency grid, as well as producing edge-lighting for the horizontal plexiglass sheets. An unexpected, but happy, result of the edge-lighting was that as the visitor walked past the booth, a bright spot seemed to move along the plex edges.

Using a grid of black anodized aluminum permitted quick changes and flexibility. Each square could hold a mirrored block or a transparency holder, or even a hinged door to provide storage space.

36 SMALL EXHIBITS

Exhibitor: Souvenir
Producer: Heritage Display Group, Dallas
Designer: Ken Konke

This small island display uses a dominant octagonal center structure which holds both transparencies and actual samples, while four corner demonstration tables hold small sample displays as well. The custom carpet helps to identify the exhibitor.

Exhibitor: NGN & Co., Rush
Producer/Designer: Visual Fabrications Inc.

The exhibitor, a manufacturer of young kids' rough and ready clothes, wanted an exhibit that would reflect that image. The clothing was shown inside the lefthand rooms, while the store was used as a conference room.

Exhibitor:	Gates Engineering
Producer:	Display Arts Studios Inc.
Designer:	Barbara A. Riggio

The design reflects the strength and solidity of the exhibitor. The waterfall tiers, shading from black to light gray, have built-in lighting. Plants add a touch of warmth to the matching literature stand along the aisle.

Exhibitor: CLD 9
Producer: Exhibitgroup, San Francisco
Designer: Armando Orubeondo

An unusual, low-cost design using Letraset patterns for wallpaper. Forced perspective gives the illusion of more space.

Exhibitor: Jetway Systems
Producer: Skyline Displays Inc.
Designer: Dan Bianchi

To get a lightweight, portable exhibit with visual impact, the exhibitor turned to elements of the Mirage display system.

Exhibitor: L.M. Animal Farms
Producer/Designer: Downing Displays Inc.

Here a light-weight, portable, stock display is customized with woodgrain vinyl application, an authentic wood shake shingle roof, and a large photomural.

Exhibitor: Anheuser-Busch Inc.
Producer: Heritage Communications of St. Louis
Designer: Joe Hennessy

An old world rathskeller was created for a national sales conference.

Exhibitor: U S West Inc.
Producer: Exhibits Inc.
Designer: Good Show!, Inc.

Designed to reflect the humanistic management philosophy of the exhibitor, this exhibit uses hand colored photographs over a silk-screened laminate background with a fabric base.

Exhibitor: The Beef Industry Council
Producer: Exhibitgroup, San Francisco
Designer: Armando Orubeondo

An unusual touch is given by the three cut-out shapes that represent the exhibit's theme of "Morning, Noon & Night." Two cabinet units that hold back-lit transparencies serve as storage containers, and are placed three feet from the simple backwall to create visual interest.

SMALL EXHIBITS 41

Exhibitor: **Essex**
Producer: Cyclonics Inc.
Designer: Martin Spicuzza

This booth, with its clean, architectural look, was able to display a large number of wall coverings without looking cluttered by using panels along the back wall which slid on tracks.

Exhibitor: Union Bank
Producer: Universal Exhibits
Designer: Matrix Design Consultants

The design reflects the solid reputation of the exhibitor. It can be installed in a 10-foot space as well as in the 20-foot space shown.

Exhibitor: DuPont/Fibers Division
Producer: Art Guild Inc.
Designer: Van Sickle & Rolleri

The design objective was to use the product as the major visual element, and to create an upbeat, contemporary look, with fun and movement. The horizontal cylinders, covered with Tyvek, rotated slowly.

Exhibitor: United Longchamp Int. & United Exposition Service
Producer/Designer: United Longchamp Intl.

This exhibit was designed to highlight how modular exhibit systems can be used to create unusual designs. Even the waterfall was built entirely of modular components.

Exhibitor: Pennzoil, Gumout Division
Producer: Giltspur Exhibits, Pittsburgh
Designer: Cindie Bonomi

To introduce a new product, a 48-inch replica was mounted on a turntable, with actual samples on display on nearby pedestals.

46   SMALL EXHIBITS

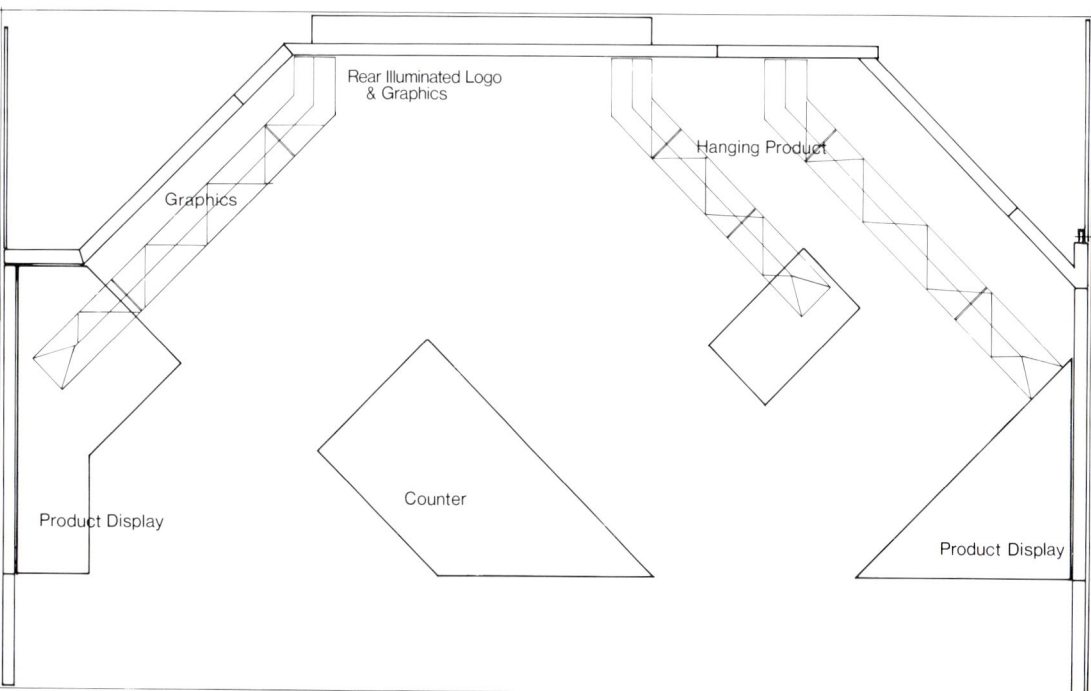

Exhibitor: Manville/Holophane Division
Producer: Design Dynamics/Exhibits
Designer: Roger M. Rios

The objectives of this exhibit were to showcase product and to present a more exciting corporate image to a younger generation of specifiers in the commercial lighting industry. Custom design, using the Interlock System, created a perfect marriage of light, darkness, and a "hot" look.

SMALL EXHIBITS 47

Exhibitor: BellSouth Services
Producer/Designer: Design South Inc.

The openness of this island exhibit and its unusual towers attracted visitors to view demonstrations and to use the interactive terminals.

Exhibitor: American Optical
Producer: The Exhibit Company
Designer: Jim Kelley

Made completely from Exponents System parts, with neon lights highlighting the three-dimensional logos on the top piece and that spell out the company slogan on two of the four kiosks. The open and visible conference area was designed to permit the new company president and otehr top management people to talk to as many visitors as possible. The free-standing plasma ball serves as an attractive conversation piece. Product was illustrated and displayed on the inside faces of the kiosks.

48 SMALL EXHIBITS

Exhibitor: R.L.I. Insurance Co.
Producer: Exhibit Source Inc.
Designer: Kirk Goltry

Using components from Exponents Inc., this 20-foot space contains three service areas and 3 computer software demos.

Exhibitor: Novatel
Producer: Geron Associates Ltd.
Designer: Ramon Brioux

Four Self-Pac displays are used as a group for an island display, but they can each be used individually. The identification sign is retractable for use under a 8-foot height limitation.

Exhibitor/Designer: Apt Display Products
Producer: Moss Exhibits

This simple background does not draw attention away from the product, and yet is easy to erect and ship.

Exhibitor:	Champion International Corp.
Producer:	Giltspur Exhibits, Boston
Designer:	Chris Kolesnik

Life-sized soft sculpture, in the theme area, created a crowd-stopping attraction, whether it was a newsstand setting for one show or a post-office for another.

Exhibitor:	Hubbell Steel Co.
Producer:	Exhibit Source Inc.
Designer:	Kirk Goltry

Rather than stress samples of the exhibitor's products, which are not very exciting, the exhibit used large, dramatic photographs. The aluminum tubes and frames of the Nimlok System tied in well with the exhibitor's galvanized sheet and coils.

SMALL EXHIBITS 51

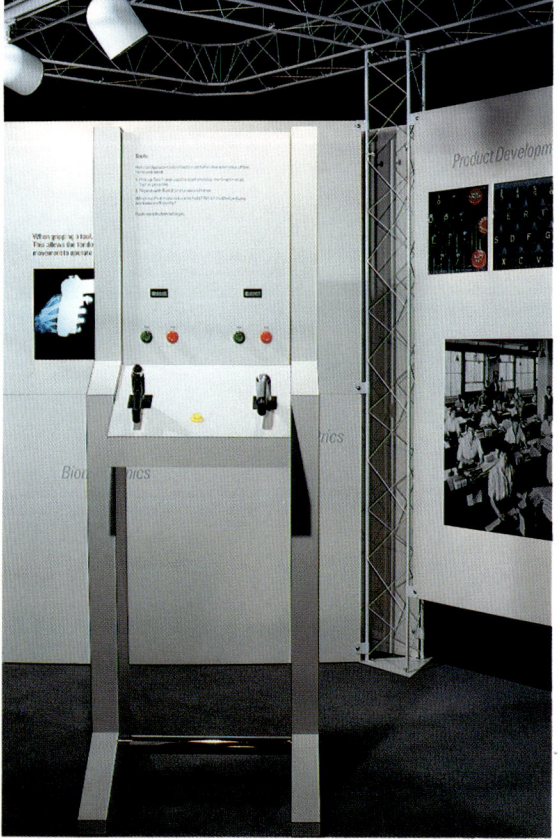

Exhibitor: IBM
Producer: Condit Exhibits
Designer: Good Show!, Inc.

Hands-on demonstrations leading visitors to discover for themselves the basic principles of ergonomic design were the key to the success of this traveling display.

52 SMALL EXHIBITS

Exhibitor: Analogic
Producer: David Brace Displays Inc.
Designer: Richard Rumsey

The large rear-lit transparencies are set in gray Formica, with ½-inch bent plexiglass used for separators and counters. Glowing shelves, transparencies, pierced lettering, and louvre-directed downlight utilizes lighting to its fullest.

Exhibitor: Vistakon
Producer: Dimension Works
Designer: Fred Svetlik

An elegant, eye-catching exhibit was created through the use of chrome, suede fabrics, and transparencies.

Exhibitor: Massingill, Division of Beecham Products
Producer: Giltspur Exhibits, Pittsburgh
Designer: Dorothea Langley

This essentially is a 10-foot unit which can be extended with two wings to fit a 20-foot space. A 6' × 2' illuminated header calls attention to the main graphics, and a 6-inch baffle covered with the same bronze, metallic veneer serves to throw soft illumination onto a sloped counter surface on which literature is displayed.

Exhibitor: The Southern Company
Producer/Designer: Sugar Creek Studios Inc.

Special neon lightning bolts call attention to this exhibit, created with Max system elements. It has a finished back, so it can be used in a free-standing location.

Exhibitor: Cardio Data Systems Inc.
Producer: Design Realizations Inc.
Designer: George L. Down

The clean lines of this exhibit combine a sense of solidity with the style of a forward-looking, technologically advanced medical company.

Exhibitor: Keller Manufacturing
Producer/Designer: Pingel Displays Inc.

High product visibility, coupled with strong company signage is blended with earth tones in the backwall, the furnishings, and the carpet. Easy hands-on capability.

Exhibitor: Digital Research Inc.
Producer: Skyline Displays Inc.
Designer: Les LaMotte

A totally portable exhibit, this is designed for use at small shows and seminars, and is able to show all of the exhibitor's software options.

Exhibitor: Digital Research Inc.
Producer: Skyline Displays Inc.
Designer: Les LaMotte

Exhibitor: Minners Designs
Producer/Designer: Graphic Displays

The nature of the products required a lot of display cases, with good lighting for maximum impact. Black cases, with slat-wall backs, permitted many different arrangements of glass shelves, with low-voltage lighting. The elements can easily be set up for 10, 20 or 30 lineal foot exhibits, using various combinations of elements.

Exhibitor: Hills Bros Coffee Companies
Producer/Designer: TGA Displays Inc.

Three designs were developed, one for each of the coffee brands owned by the exhibitor, plus a corporate design incorporating all three logos. Each of them could be attached to a universal background. Multiple sets were prepared by silkscreen for use in regional shows around the country. The structures are from Nomadic, using gold end caps to give the system a polished, finished look.

CHAPTER 3
Medium Exhibits

A little more room, a little more money, a little more challenge, a little more opportunity—that's what the examples in this chapter have in common. Here the space, especially as you reach the upper limit of the indicated range, require the designer to consider the interrelationships within the parts of the exhibit, and the varied functions it must serve. There is more variety, more different approaches, than we saw in the previous chapter.

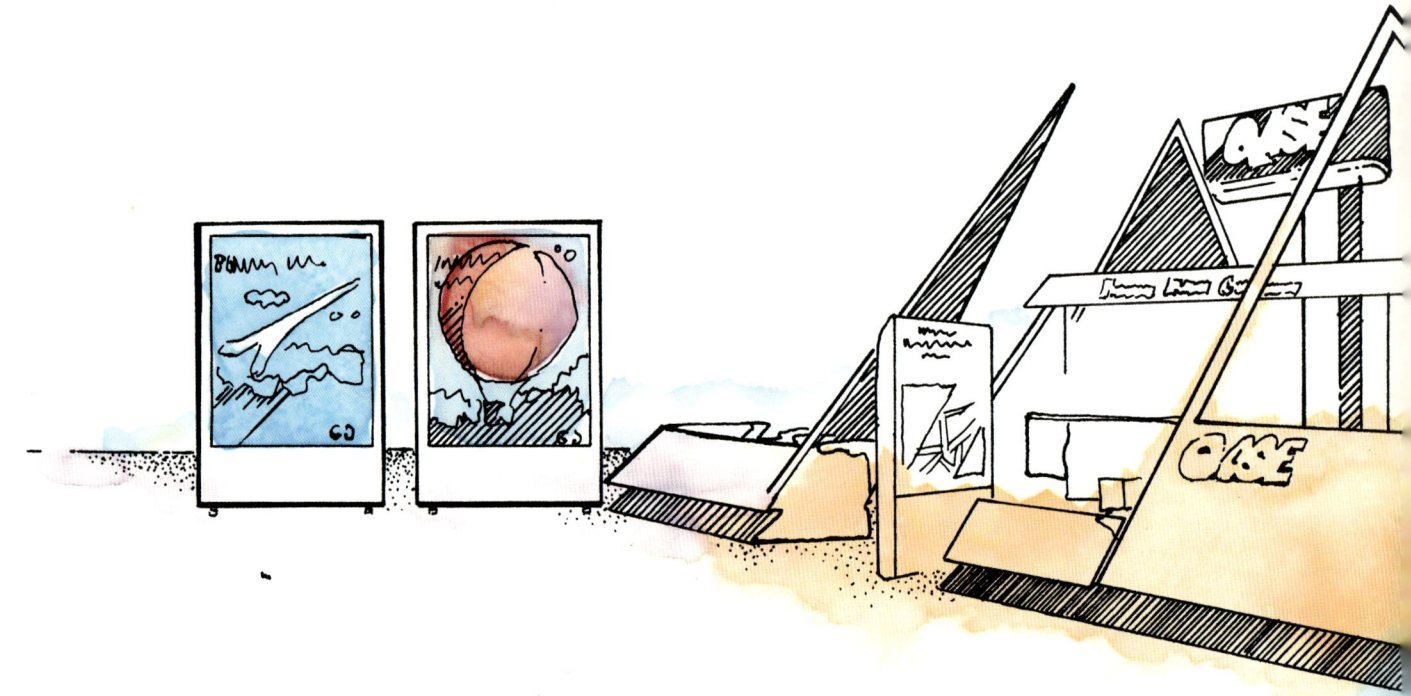

Exhibitor: Vulcan
Producer/Designer: Expoglass Sistemas Modulares

Building the design around the exhibitor's initial, but inverted, highlights the entrance area. This 16-foot structure, using Octanorm elements was furnished on a rental basis.

Exhibitor: Eastman Kodak Co./Clinical Products Div.
Producer/Designer: Impact Exhibits Inc.

This custom-designed rental exhibit was produced to project the company's worldwide identity in major European fairs. The logotype tower, positions in the front of the exhibit, provides excellent visibility.

Exhibitor:	Empire Pencil Co.
Producer:	Matrix Exhibits
Designer:	Raymond Watkins

Ten-foot replicas of the company's most familiar product are mounted to the walls of the two octagonal conference rooms in this island space.

MEDIUM EXHIBITS 61

Exhibitor:	Pfizer Pigments Div.
Producer:	Presentations South Inc.
Designer:	Robert McGarry; John Cunitz

The operating machine that mixes pigment needs water, drains, compressed air and electric lines, and the exhibit had to be designed to assemble during a single shift to permit fine-tuning the demonstration gear.

Exhibitor:	Sanitaire
Producer/Designer:	Hartwig Exhibitions

These self-standing modules can be used independently, back-to-back or in tandem, with large transparencies telling the in-depth story. The shape of the headers suggests a water conduit.

Exhibitor: Molex Incorporated
Producer: Kitzing Incorporated
Designer: Fred Kitzing

Welded stainless steel rod components provided a skeletal framework that supported stretched nylon fabric. Rising to a height of 16-feet, the framework supported counters, conference walls and product transparencies as though they were floating.

Exhibitor: ADC Telecommunications
Producer: Heritage Display Group, St. Paul
Designer: Jack Schneider

This exhibit, with a strong visual impact, suggests the interconnectivity of telecommunications. The hanging logos give good identification.

MEDIUM EXHIBITS 63

Exhibitor:	American Wood Council
Producers:	Exhibit Design Consultants; All West Display
Designer:	Joe Maricich; Rick Riday; Tony Reynolds; Matt Rothan

This exhibit was a joint project for the four associations that make up the client, and was designed to illustrate modern techniques of wood homebuilding construction. The main structure, showing this, was on the back wall, and each association had its individual kiosk and meeting area, connected to the main structure across a wood deck.

Exhibitor: Corning Glass
Producer: Click Systems Ltd.
Designer: Michael Orr

A ceiling grid on 2-foot centers, set on a diagonal to the walls, made this a particularly challenging design, capable of configuration in 20, 30 and 40-foot spaces.

Exhibitor: Classical Optical
Producer/Designer: Adex Inc.

The Stonehenge theme was utilized because of its classical feeling and its prestige. Seating areas were used for inspection of the frames and writing orders. The stone surface forms an interesting background for the product.

Exhibitor: IEEE
Producer: Heritage Display Group, Dallas
Designer: Ken Konke

These standard units can be placed in many configurations, and permit visitors easy access to literature.

Exhibitor: Gulpen Beer Brewery
Producer: Oscar Chiaradia Studios
Designer: Oscar Chiaradia Studios

The design of this exhibit is patterned after a farmhouse from the region in which the exhibitor is located.

66   MEDIUM EXHIBITS

Exhibitor:	National Olympic Committee—Sofia
Producer/Designer:	Plan 3 GmbH

Using white powder-coated Octanorm extrusions, white panels and a white floor, in a very futuristic design, Sofia promotes itself for the 1992 Winter Olympics.

Exhibitor:	Bunge Corporation
Producer/Designer:	Convention Exhibits Inc.

This island exhibit is based on a newly-developed, inexpensive, but high quality 10 stock custom structure. All graphics and headers are easily changed.

MEDIUM EXHIBITS 67

Exhibitor: American Heart Association
Producer: Freeman Design Display
Designer: Rick Gronenfeld

Made up of a number of 10' × 10' sections which can be used individually, this is built of lightweight materials, and is simple to install and dismantle.

Exhibitor: Royal Doulton
Producer/Designer: Exhibits International

A unique implementation of the Octanorm system, especially in the diamond-shaped back wall. The lighting was incorporated into the panels, giving a large amount of merchandising space.

Exhibitor:	Software Design & Management
Producer:	Ausstellungsbau Klaus Woerdehoff
Designer:	Klaus Woerdehoff

Wide open entrance areas invited visitors to enter, where their first contacts were made at tables. For more private meetings, three conference rooms were available. The structure uses green powder-coated Octanorm extrusions, with white panels.

Exhibitor: ICI Americas Inc.
Producer: Display Arts Studios Inc.
Designer: Emil A Mellow II

The curving of the wings, made up of internally illuminated display cabinets, keeps an open feeling in this linear booth. On either side of the rotating hexagonal cabinet in the rear, seen against a mirrored tamboured wall, is a small conference room.

Exhibitor: Hoechst-Roussel Pharmaceuticals Inc.
Producer/Designer: Adex Inc.

To get maximum visitor involvement, this booth was designed with a central identification structure, surrounded by a varying combination of interactive computer work stations and detailing desks. As many as 30 computer carrels and 6 detailing stations could be accommodated.

Exhibitor: Sweats/Fizz Ed.
Producer/Designer: Visual Fabrications Inc.

Use of stretched canvas and exposed metalwork gave the exhibitor the connection with the athletic look.

Exhibitor: General DataComm
Producer/Designer: Sugar Creek Studios Inc.

The differently-colored headers conveyed the idea of networking, and distinguished each division's display, while it tied the whole company together.

Exhibitor: Donohoe O'Brien & Associates
Producer: T. L. Horton Design Inc.
Designer: Henry Smith; Cheri Morris

Behind formal arches, framed drawings seem to float against illuminated walls, mounted on plastic bubbles.

Exhibitor: Tempo
Producer: Heritage Display Group, Dallas
Designer: Ken Konke

Four separate programming services had to be isolated, with a strong logo visibility.

Exhibitor: Pierce Foods
Producer: ExpoSystems
Designer: S. Laird Jenkins Corp.

To afford the greatest exposure to visitors, a multiscreen modular display system was designed as an island booth, allowing traffic to flow past the counters that offered a wide range of product samples, and corporate literature. Food was prepared within the irregularly-shaped counter, which also had concealed storage space. A Rotographics unit was used to show how one of the products looked after two methods of preparation.

MEDIUM EXHIBITS 73

Exhibitor:	Bard Cardiology Division
Producer:	Innovations Inc.
Designer:	David Malas

Interesting curved shapes, with hanging vertical banners, serve to draw attention to this exhibit with its large transparencies and a small conference area.

Exhibitor:	World Book
Producer:	Cyclonics Inc.
Designer:	Martin Spicuzza

A variety of spaces is formed in this display, to emphasize the three learning levels of software offered by the exhibitor.

Exhibitor: Glaxo Inc.
Producer/Designer: Sugar Creek Studios Inc.

The exhibitor asked for an interesting architectural look: open, linear, and soft, but very modern. There is a partially enclosed conference room, and unusual cantilevered detail desks.

Exhibitor:	Burroughs-Wellcome Co.
Producer:	Giltspur Exhibits, Boston
Designer:	John Barrett

To introduce a new drug, three stages of communication were included in this exhibit. There was a double-montage video production facing two opposite aisles, to provide an overview. Individual interactive computer stations, with touch screens, provided in-depth information for doctors, and there was a conference area and detail counters for one-to-one interaction.

Exhibitor: Pratt & Lambert
Producer: Kitzing Incorporated
Designers: Fred Kitzing; Ross Thompson

The highlight of this exhibit was a full-scale replica of a paint store circa 1849, designed to emphasize the company's stability, control and long-term commitment to the independent paint dealer. The store served also as a background for taking Polaroid photographs of show attendees.

MEDIUM EXHIBITS 77

Exhibitor: Herlitz Inc.
Producer: Skyline Displays Inc.
Designers: Robert Gambrel; Mike Boyce

A series of self standing units, using Mirage components, serve to display both a large photographic mural and hold a series of display racks.

Exhibitor: Medical Incorporated
Producer: Exhibitgroup Chicago
Designer: Rick Lewis

Within a space frame, graphics are presented in a dramatic way utilizing handmade infinity mirrors, creating an effect of infinite space within a few inches of real space. Integrated is a fiber optic display which creates a repeated oscilloscope wave simulating the human heart beat.

Exhibitor: Astra Pharmaceutical Products Inc.
Producer: Giltspur Exhibits, Pittsburgh
Designer: Dottie Clark

In an effort to suggest the company's new headquarters, the custom modules were designed with straight backs and sloped fronts, which suggested a pyramid. This was strengthened by the truncated pyramidal Meroform structure that was used as a ceiling and to support the company name, made of 18-inch plexi letters outlined with neon lights. Feature demonstrations take place inside the pyramid, where they are taped and shown on six monitors placed near the selling stations near the aisles.

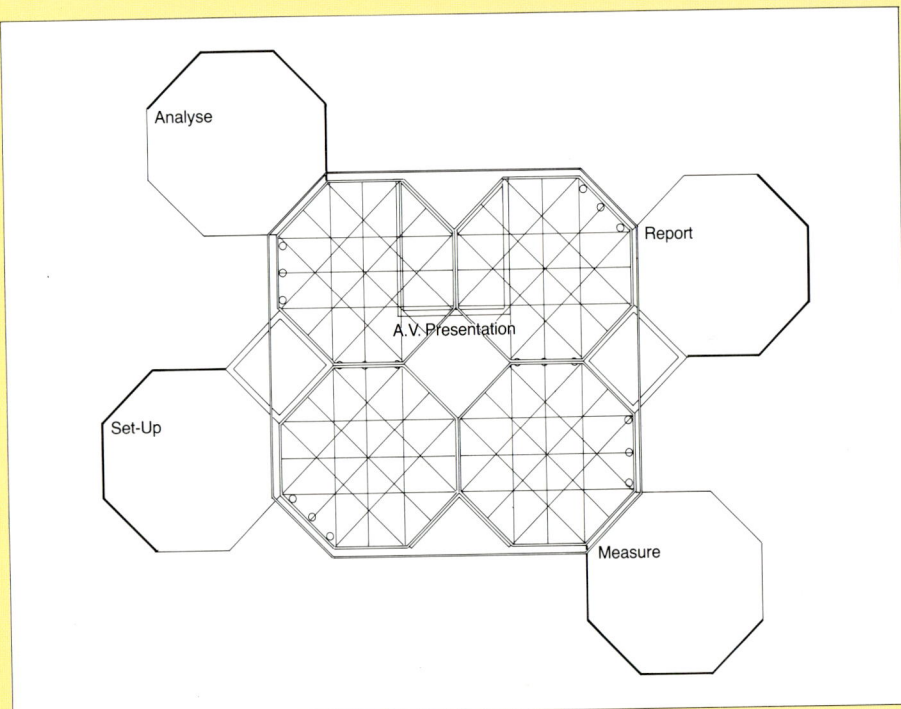

Exhibitor:	Honeywell Test Management Systems
Producer:	Design Dynamics, Exhibits
Designer:	Roger M. Rios

Semi-private demo rooms radiate off an overhead identification structure whose honeycomb hexagons suggest the corporate identity.

Exhibitor:	Smead Manufacturing
Producer:	Haas Display Co.
Designer:	Darold Johnson

These two triangular structures, each 12-foot high, provided high identification and a feeling of mass. Twelve small display windows were built into each of the two units and showed product, while interior windows featured a pictorial history of the 80-year-old company.

MEDIUM EXHIBITS 81

CHAPTER  Large Exhibits

Following the lead of the IEA's Focus Awards, we adopted four size categories and devoted a chapter to each, but I would like to point out that there is no sharp contrast from one category to the next, but a steadily increasing complexity as you move up in size. Thus, this chapter which I have called "large," includes bigger, more complex, and bigger budgeted examples of designers' work. The larger space is designed to display more product and attract more people. It more often has a sit-down theater for live or recorded presentations, as well as more space for conference rooms.

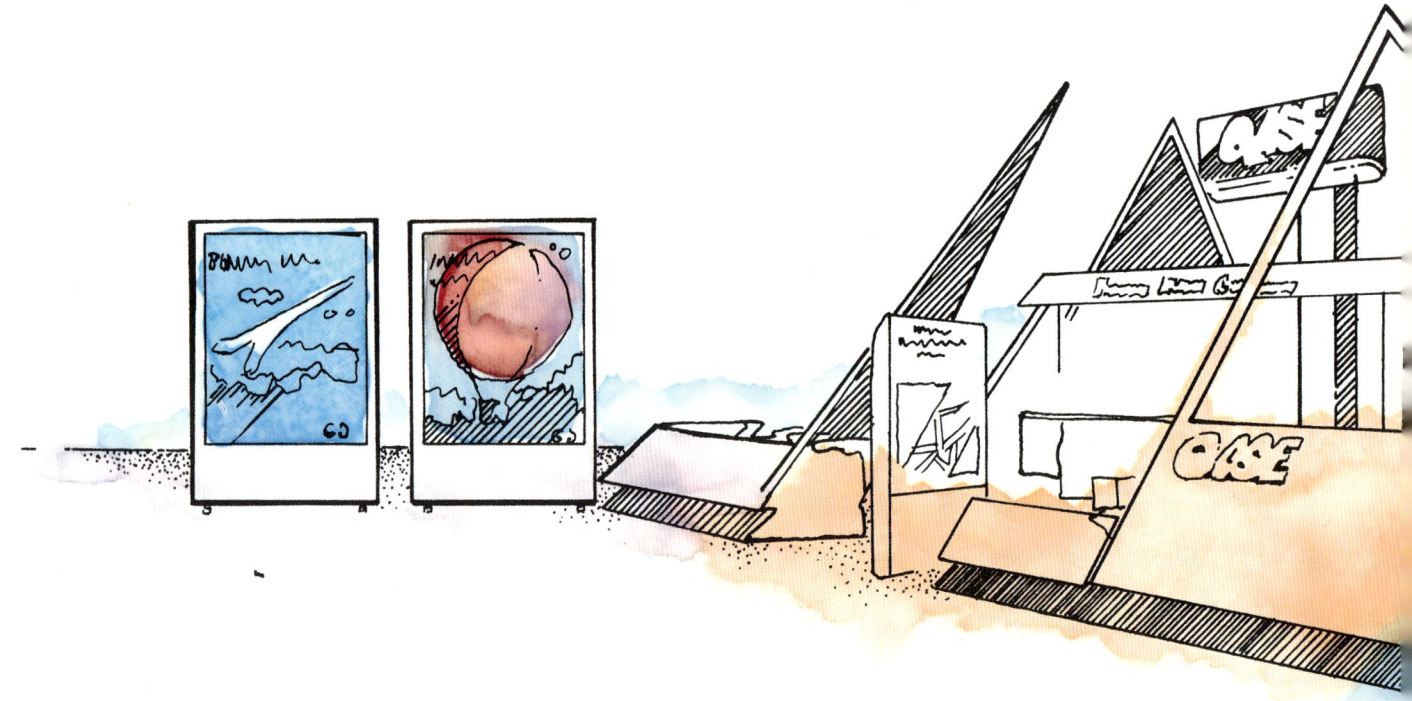

Exhibitor: DePuy Inc.
Producer: Gallo Displays Inc.
Designer: Al Russell

Many of the elements in this large exhibit could be used independently for smaller shows, as could virtually all the graphics. Demonstrations could be made both one-on-one and to large groups. A special feature of this exhibit was a number of stations where surgeons could review and select videotapes on surgical procedures.

Exhibitor: Pioneer Communications
Producer: Boss Display Corporation
Designer: Bill Tucker; Bill Bennett

In order to reduce installation costs, this exhibit consisted of modules on casters, each 2' × 5' × 8'. Each module included all the equipment for a complete two-channel television station, which was pre-packed and pre-loaded prior to the show, reducing on-floor installation and wiring costs.

Exhibitor: Du Pont Corian
Producer: Art Guild Inc.
Designer: Van Sickle & Rolleri

The exhibitor's objective was to create a selling environment that establishes Corian as a market leader in the home building and home remodeling fields. Small room sets were interspersed with technical sections, bringing contractors and designers face to face with actual applications, giving both the how and why of the product.

Exhibitor: Case Communications
Producer: Production House Inc.
Designer: Design Plus Two Inc.

The truncated and outlined pyramids which define the space used for this exhibit are so distinctive that not only has it attracted attention on the floor, but it has been adopted by the exhibitor as a symbol and is used on its promotional pieces.

LARGE EXHIBITS 85

Exhibitor: Ricoh Corp.
Producer/Designer: Impact Exhibits Inc.

This is the 40′ × 50′ configurations of an exhibit which can be set up from 30′ × 30′ to 150′ × 50′. Included are a 20 foot tower, two conference rooms, seven selling areas, and a 140 square foot storage room.

Exhibitor:	Konica Medical Corporation
Producer:	Exhibitgroup, Chicago
Designer:	Rick Lewis

A rotating sign, 8 feet in diameter, made this exhibit easy to locate from almost anywhere in the vast exhibit hall. In addition, plexiglass bands on the upper deck conference area provided privacy.

LARGE EXHIBITS 87

Exhibitor:	Crissa Corporation
Producer:	McCormick Display
Designers:	Dan Burk; Alain Couture

An elegant combination of black marble, frosted glass, dramatic lighting and muted wine hues concentrated the visitor's attention on the product display. Lighting and a focused traffic flow improves visibility and creates an excitement about the product and the company.

Exhibitor:	Uniforms to You
Producer:	Dimension Works
Designer:	Fred Svetlik

This 30' × 65' cross-aisle exhibit was constructed out of galvanized steel cat walk panels welded together to give a funky, hi-tech feeling. Hot pink fluorescent lights within the steel and the checkerboard center aisle carpet added to the exhibit's fashion show feeling.

Exhibitor:	Clark Equipment Co.
Producer:	Rowe Thomas Displays
Designer:	Stuart Stone

The floor space was divided into quadrants by four towers which incorporated screens for audio-visual presentations, designed to visually move the audience from one quadrant to the next where the product was physically demonstrated.

LARGE EXHIBITS 89

Exhibitor:	Dennison National
Producer:	Exhibitgroup, New York
Designer:	George Raustiala

Two companion exhibits set up dancing fountains directly opposite the main entrance to the show floor. The raised platform, floating on a perimeter light, housed a number of modular demonstration and product areas, conference rooms, and a small stage. Natural wood ceilings gave warmth to the construction and permitted pin-point lighting control.

Exhibitor: Bissell
Producer: Exponents Inc., George P. Johnson Co.
Designer: Kenneth Jamieson

This large exhibit, consisting of two 20′ × 90′ spaces facing each other across an aisle, combined stock components with custom-made additions to give an exhibit with lots of demonstration areas around the edges of the two central structures and a large number of semi-private conference rooms. The upper structure gave excellent corporate identity and conference rooms for four of the company's divisions.

Exhibitor:	Equity Properties & Development Co.
Producer:	T.L. Horton Design Inc.
Designers:	Jim Connor; Tim Smith; Tony Horton; Cheri Morris

The exhibit was made almost entirely of brightly colored, over-scaled shopping bags to give the exhibitor a strong retail image. This theme was tied into a magazine ad and a direct mail piece.

Exhibitor: Goodman Segar Hogan
Producer: T.L. Horton Design Inc.
Designer: Tony Horton

A custom wall panel system gives a clean and spacious air, with plenty of room for conference areas.

Exhibitor: Johnson & Johnson Orthopedic Div.
Producer: Admore Inc.
Designer: Charles McMillian

The white, building-block effect was softened by an adobe texture, creative illumination and greenery. Highlight of the exhibit was a recording studio where physicians could prepare their own introductions to J&J videotapes explaining orthopedic procedures to patients.

Exhibitor: Sandoz Pharmaceutical
Producer: Giltspur Exhibits, Boston
Designer: John Barrett

The free standing units could be positioned to fill a variety of spaces, including islands 20' × 40', 20' × 30', 40' × 60'. Strong identification is achieved by the use of towers, and the graphic area can easily be varied. The central sand sculpture, created during the shows, kept people coming back to watch progress.

Exhibitor: Hoechst Chemicals
Producer: Oscar Chiaradia Studios
Designer: Oscar Chiaradia Studios

This exhibit was built for the distribution of the national 1987 Dutch Renovation prizes for older buildings. The tower is 25 feet tall.

LARGE EXHIBITS 95

Exhibitor: Samuel Goldwyn
Producer: Matrix Exhibits
Designer: Brendan McDonnell

This exhibit included four screening rooms and a food bar within its 12-foot high curved walls.

Exhibitor: YKK Zippers Inc.
Producer: Sugar Creek Studios Inc.
Designer: David Langston

Machinery at work formed the highlight of this exhibit, with a new advertising campaign dramatically displayed in lightboxes in the cantilevered headers.

LARGE EXHIBITS   97

Exhibitor: Dr. Pepper
Producer: Heritage Display Group, Dallas
Designer: Ken Konke

Two products shared this space, with Welch's being constructed with the Product Presentation system, so that it could be shown by itself for smaller shows. While the major part of the area was devoted to project sampling in a fun setting, conference areas were also included.

Exhibitor: Coca Cola U.S.A.
Producer: C. Henning Studios Inc.
Designer: Cassandra Henning

A facade, replicating a 1930 style storefront design, was installed at the entrance to the exhibit area for the Coca Cola Centennial celebration. The windows held antique window displays and other memorabilia. The entire structure was self-supporting, since no rigging or support points were readily available.

Exhibitor: Revere Ware Inc.
Producer: Kitzing Incorporated
Designer: Joseph Panzarella

It is sometimes a problem to convey the image of tradition and innovation, but this exhibit succeeded by using giant copper logos, rising from a blue plexiglass, oak-trimmed structure, combined with exciting lighting of product displays which dramatically reflected the chrome and copper products. Multi-level conference areas were built to provide a quiet place to do business.

Exhibitor: Harcourt Brace Jovanovich
Producer: Giltspur Exhibits, Pittsburgh
Designer: Dorothea Langley

Double-sided modular units, using the Meroform system, were designed to provide easy product viewing and sampling by show visitors. Demo units for interactive computer programs and seating units with hidden storage interface with the modular units to add versatility. The overhead Meroform structure lends a touch of elegance, and provides a large identification area for the HBJ trademark.

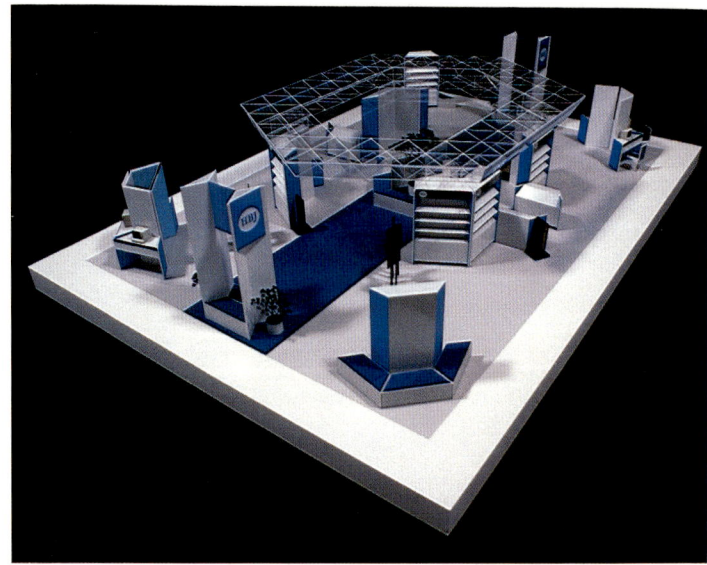

Exhibitor: Star Micronics Inc.
Producer: Giltspur Exhibits, Rochester
Designer: Mark Norenberg

Most of the attention is focused on the product through the use of interesting shapes, colors, and finishes. A modular approach permitted the display to be used in a variety of configurations. The free standing modules permitted easy accessibility to all products.

Exhibitor: Schwinn Bicycle Co.
Producer: Kitzing Incorporated
Designers: Fred Kitzing; Dean Showalter

This exhibit was designed to show a model bicycle store. It included a simulated brick facade, with front and side doors, bay windows, and good identification.

Exhibitor: Camex
Producer: Fahey Exhibits
Designer: Paul Occhipinti

The audio-visual demonstration area faced the front of the booth, while the lead desk was set behind, encouraging front-to-back traffic flow, which was assisted by closing the sides. There were five major demo areas and two conference rooms.

Exhibitor:	Digital Equipment Corp.
Producer:	Giltspur Exhibits, Boston
Designer:	Jane Corbus

Speaking to an audience of bankers, the booth replicated a competely networked banking environment, using cut-away walls, open portal entrances and change in carpet color to create the illusion of five separate banking establishments. There were office-like settings for 12 different manned demonstrations throughout the exhibit.

LARGE EXHIBITS 103

Exhibitor: Pentax
Producer: Exhibit by Design
Designer: Jeff Burke

The low counters, with truss ceilings overhead, kept a feeling of openness, while the enclosed spaces along two sides of the area gave room for conference rooms, one of which was totally enclosed, and for demonstration areas.

Exhibitor: The Upjohn Company
Producer: Design Craftsmen Inc.
Designer: Karl Utrecht

Utilizing the Mark III Modular Exhibit System, the key element is a rectangular arch that can be installed in various shapes and heights to lend variety and yet maintain continuity of design. Rear-lit transparencies can be mounted on pedestals that mirror the shape of the arches, or on light boxes that mount between the arches.

Exhibitor:	Dallas Corporation
Producer:	Heritage Display Group, Dallas
Designer:	Ken Konke

With products for the building industry ranging from garage doors to thermal windows, being shown in varied combinations from one show to another, the designer developed some freestanding columns that served for identification and space definition. The products were mounted on specially-built truss frames that helped unify the space.

Exhibitor:	Klockner Pentaplast
Producer:	Display Art Studios Inc.
Designer:	Barbara A. Riggio

To avoid the monotony of a long in-line exhibit, the back wall is broken up here by a conference room at each end, plus a large storage room in the center. Special display cabinets light products from underneath. Since there were operating machines, all the cabinets had to be covered to protect the contents from dust.

LARGE EXHIBITS 105

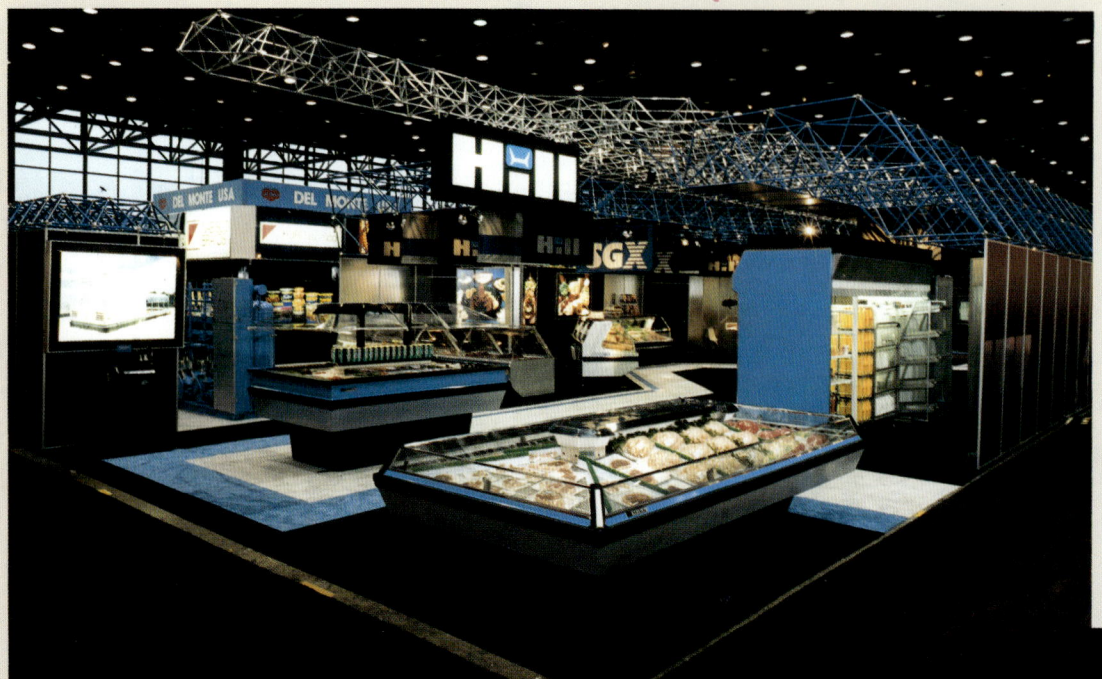

Exhibitor: Hill Refrigeration Corp.
Producer/Designer: United Longchamp International

The exhibitor likes to change his color and style each year to suggest that its product can be customized. Special carpeting and wallcolors on standard systems, rented each year, ties the exhibit together with the equipment. The overhead truss system also helps to unify the display.

106 LARGE EXHIBITS

Exhibitor: Jaguar
Producer: Exhibitgroup, New York
Designer: Alex Karpilov

The highlight of this exhibit designed to introduce a new line was a large turntable with bold company identification. Further identification was given by the large standing signs at each corner.

LARGE EXHIBITS 107

Exhibitor: Pellon Corporation
Producer/Designer: Sugar Creek Studios

Designed as an active order-writing booth, the exhibit faced inward to discourage casual traffic. The smoked plastic shields on top of the structures helped to control noise and increase privacy without adding a feeling of seclusion. The illuminated world map in the center rotated.

Exhibitor: Wetrok Cleaning Supplies
Producer: Oscar Chiaradia Studios
Designer: Oscar Chiaradia Studios

The complete header structure is suspended from the four main pillars.

Exhibitor:	Digital Communications Associates Inc.
Producer:	Sugar Creek Studios Inc.
Designer:	John Lander

A number of free-standing towers create an interesting space, tempting to explore. Visual presentations and graphic displays involve the visitor.

LARGE EXHIBITS 109

Exhibitor: Pacific Bell
Producer/Designer: Bluepeter

The exhibitor wanted a system that looked hi-tech and could handle a wide variety of sizes and markets, covering 53 different shows in a year. The elements were made of white metal tube frames, brushed aluminum panels, and red neon with an open, spidery look. Units were crated separately, so that when an exhibit was needed, the desired crates could be specified, graphics added, and the needs met simply.

Exhibitor: Atlantic Aviation
Producer: Art Guild Inc.
Designer: Van Sickle & Rolleri

It was difficult to put an airplane in the exhibit space, so Atlantic Aviation showed its services with large pictures and an over-large, cut-out figure. The overhead structure tied the display units together.

LARGE EXHIBITS 111

CHAPTER  Giant Exhibits

Here are the giants of the trade show industry. They present unusual challenges to the designer, for they occur rarely in any single designer's career. Thus, it is hard to build on experience. In addition, most of them do not occur very frequently on any exhibitor's schedule. That means that each new giant exhibit is almost a brand new problem to both client and designer/producer. Understanding derived from smaller booths cannot always be extrapolated to these biggies, and the lessons you learn through putting together one such exhibit are often forgotten by the time the next challenge rolls around.

Because these major structures occur so rarely, there is almost always an attempt to design in such a way that several smaller exhibits can be put together using the elements of the giant booth, this pressure sometimes inhibits the creativity of the designer, and keeps him from taking full advantage of the space with which he is provided.

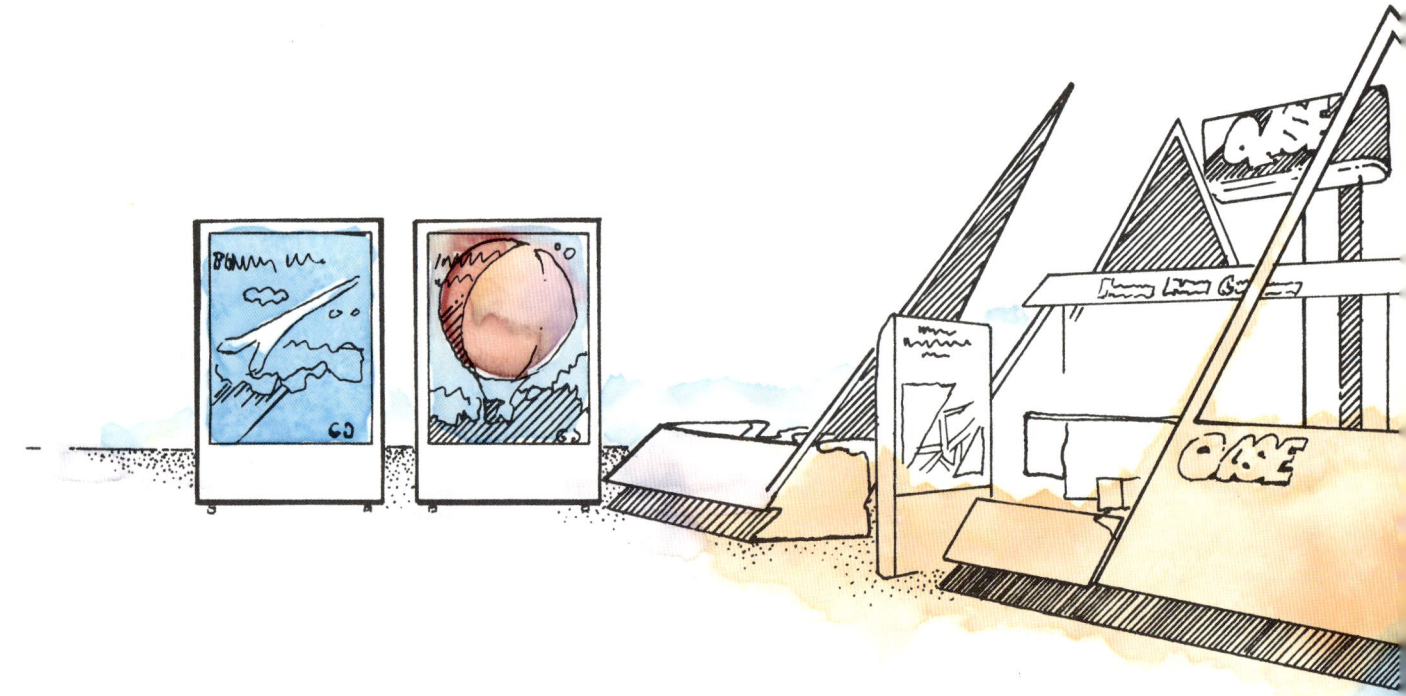

Exhibitor:	Homart Development Co.
Producer:	T.L. Horton Design Inc.
Designer:	Jim Connor

High glass surfaces, neon, and bright accent colors were incorporated to produce a polished high tech exhibit. Large scale graphics were displayed as backlighted transparencies and color murals. An office system with interchangeable components was designed to supply offices for 20 leasing reps. Smoked plexiglass panels made up the front of each office, giving privacy while providing an open environment.

GIANT EXHIBITS 115

116 GIANT EXHIBITS

Exhibitor: Crown American
Producer: T.L. Horton Design Inc.
Designer: Tony Horton

A dramatic Roman entry was used to highlight this exhibit. Realistic substitutes for stone and marble gave a feeling of permanence to the display. Post-modern components along the perimeter of the interior space displayed dimensional site lease plan graphics. Care was taken to give the interior of the exhibit a spacious feeling, accentuated by the large palms and open arches.

Exhibitor: Melvin Simon & Associates
Producer: T.L. Horton Design Inc.
Designer: Tony Horton

Soft textures, subdued lighting, an art gallery and a beautiful courtyard dining area are but a few elements used to create this 12,000 square foot exhibit. The Gallery Showroom located in the center of the exhibit displayed a collection of shopping center renderings presented in an impressionistic style. Twenty-five conference rooms were located behind the gallery to provide a place for private meetings. More informal areas were located in each side of the gallery. A lavish food service was set up in the middle of a beautiful courtyard dining area.

GIANT EXHIBITS 117

GIANT EXHIBITS 119

Exhibitor: Herring Marathon Group
Producer: T.L. Horton Design Inc.
Designer: Tony Horton

This movie theater entry exhibit was fabricated complete with chase lights, marquee and a revolving logo high atop a column of multi-colored neon. Removable letters were used on the marquee to change the now showing attraction on a daily basis. The highly visible neon was easily seen from any location on the exhibit floor. The theater theme was also used in a direct mail piece, a magazine ad, and in the giveaways.

Exhibitor: Rockwell International
Producer: Zenit Werbund
Designer: G. Gerber

In a structure of Octanorm elements that suggested a UFO, Rockwell supported its technologically advanced position. The floor level and general information about the company and its products, while the second level offered several elegant conference rooms for serious business discussions.

Exhibitor: AT&T Network Systems
Producer: Kevmar
Designer: Plumb Design Group

The concept of a switching network was protrayed with the half-round blue arch, a theme which dominated the entire exhibit. For demonstration, there were four infrared-controlled, interactive displays, bas relief cityscapes sculpted in plastic. A 16-monitor video wall was the main feature on the outside of the theater wall.

Exhibitor:	NEC Information Systems
Producer:	Giltspur Exhibits, Boston
Designer:	Waldemar Wittler

To symbolize the places in which the equipment would be used, three towers suggesting office buildings were used. Each is adjustable in height from 14 to 18 feet. The red lighting on the towers pulsate at precise intervals, giving the impression of communication. The platforms provide individuals demonstration areas, and facilitate the routing of cabling and wiring, since these can be drawn through individual doors in each platform, permitting the installation of equipment to begin earlier.

Exhibitor: AT&T
Producer/Designer: Impact Exhibits Inc.

The purpose of this 50′ × 110′ structural systems exhibit was to show dramatically how network services and equipment interface with each other. The area is marked with eight 16-foot towers with internally-illuminated logos, a fiber-optic telemarketing display, and an enclosed video teleconferencing room.

Exhibitor: Brown Boveri Corporation
Producer/Designer: Impact Exhibits Inc.

The upper-level conference areas are reached by two spiral staircases. Designed for a show that is held every 30 months, the unit is rented.

GIANT EXHIBITS 123

Exhibitor: Abbott Laboratories
Producer/Designer: Impact Exhibits Inc.

Over the entrances to the central, semi-isolated conference rooms, the three tubes with chase lights symbolize dramatically the re-oxygenation of blood. Product information is carried on 32-inch monitors in the walls of the central unit, while there are four carrels, each with its own interactive touch screen linked to laser videodisks.

Exhibitor:	Sun Chemical Corp.
Producer/Designer:	Impact Exhibits Inc.

This exhibit, 47 × 42-feet and 18-inches high, has an information center, a communications center, and eight conference rooms on the ground level, in addition to the large meeting area on the second level.

GIANT EXHIBITS 125

Exhibitor:	Mori Seiki USA
Producer:	The Derse Company
Designer:	John Anderson

This partially-enclosed booth had entrances on two corners, with many stations for demonstrating machinery. The floor plan was designed to build a good traffic flow.

Exhibitor:	Mitsui Machine Tool Sales Inc.
Producer:	The Derse Company
Designer:	John Anderson

A sales company, the exhibitor represents four tool builders, who had to be identifiable as separate entities, but yet be unified under a single banner.

Exhibitor:	Cherry-Burrell
Producer:	Exhibitgroup, Chicago
Designer:	Allan McVey

To launch a new line of packaging machines and ice cream freezers, this exhibit maximized visitor involvement through demonstrations and supporting graphics. Seven private conference areas were available for sales closings or technical meetings. Walls were designed with alcoves for customer products that had been processed or packed on the exhibitor's equipment. In addition, lightboxes showed product installations and technical flow diagrams.

128 GIANT EXHIBITS

Exhibitor: GMC Truck
Producer: Exhibitgroup, Chicago
Designer: Rick Lewis

A series of self-standing units were tied together with a truss ceiling. Highlight of the show was a live musical presentation.

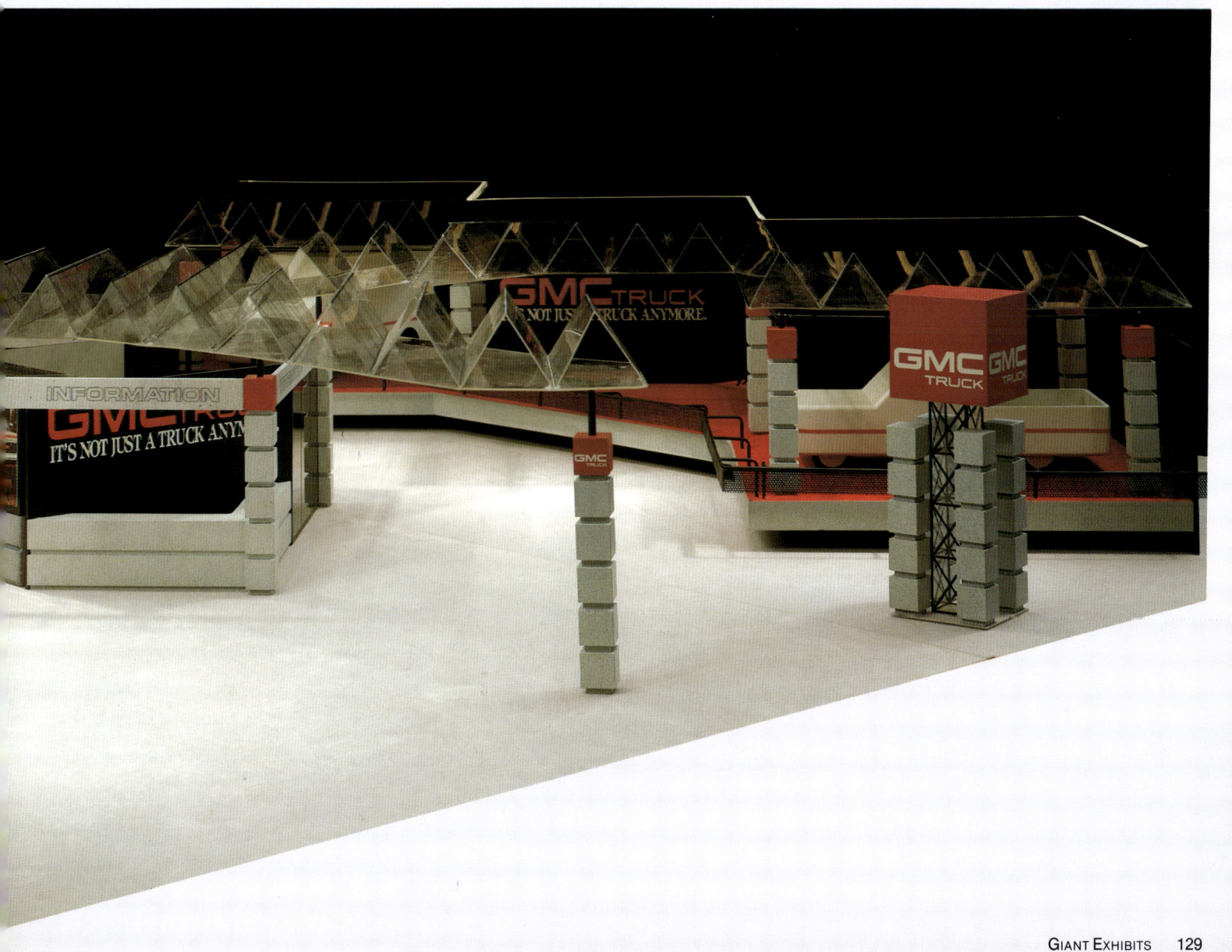

GIANT EXHIBITS 129

Exhibitor:	Volkswagen United States Inc.
Producer:	Giltspur Exhibits/Pittsburgh
Designers:	Barney Monger; Chris Wendel

The design had to be adaptable to spaces which ranged from 5,400 to 12,000 square feet, and yet be simple to set up and dismantle. An interesting feature is the raised illuminated floor which helped to high-light some of the demonstration cars.

Exhibitor:	Nissan
Producer:	George P. Johnson Co.
Designer:	Doug Johnson

To add excitement, a novel way of demonstrating a car was developed. The car in the central theme area sat on a moving light track. At a designated time, lights began a programmed sequence of flashing, as smoke billowed up from a platform capsule directly in front of the car. A man from the future emerged from the capsule and came down into the audience, inviting them to experience a vicarious ride with him through a videotape played as multi-vision on eight monitors flanking the vehicle. In addition to communicating the experience of driving the featured automobile, the theme center served as an attention getter, drawing large numbers of people into the space.

Exhibitor: Mitsubishi
Producer: George P. Johnson Co.
Designer: Jeff Bartle

Dramatic 4' × 8' rear-illuminated product transparencies are cantilevered off the central satellite structure, which incorporates strong identification. Modular vehicle platforms and turntables, each with individual product identification satellite structures, can be combined in a number of various configurations. A major identification structure provides a focal theme center including rear illuminated displays showing the full product line and Mitsubishi's technology story.

Exhibitor: Coca Cola USA
Producer: C. Henning Studios Inc.
Designer: Cassandra Henning

To highlight the history of Coca Cola at its Centennial Celebration, a replica of the soda fountain in Jacob's Pharmacy, where Coca Cola was first sold, was constructed in the Georgia World Congress Center ballroom. It incorporated archival materials, as well as working displensers from every decade since 1886.

Exhibitor: Coca Cola USA
Producer: C. Henning Studios Inc.
Designer: Cassandra Henning

As a part of its centennial celebration, Coca-Cola set up a 2000-seat theater as a demonstration of satellite communications which went on during the three-day event. Transmissions from six continents were produced and coordinated from a control truck in the theater. They were shown on the 64 monitor video wall on the outside, and six large screens, one for each continent, on the inside. Flanking the entrance were towers with clocks showing the time from each of the 168 countries where the product is sold.

Exhibitor:	Owens/Corning Fiberglas
Producer:	Heritage Display Group, Dallas
Designer:	Mark Weitzman

Faced with a change in plans, including a reduced budget, after a large space had been reserved, the exhibitor decided to concentrate on its theme, "Owens/Corning Performs," by highlighting a group of Olympic gymnastics in its exhibit area. The performing area was at one end of the space, with a ceiling of bright fabric banners. Television cameras and projectors hidden among the banners showed the live performance on a screen above the stage. The rest of the space was occupied by six pyramid-topped booths where visitors could talk to the performers, and sales people could talk to visitors.

134   GIANT EXHIBITS

Exhibitor:	Halliburton Companies
Producer:	Heritage Display Group, Dallas
Designer:	Ken Konke

Nine companies had to be brought together under one corporate umbrella for a major show, but each had to be able to take its portion independently to smaller shows. The solution was the development of a series of modular units built around a standard frame which could hold various combinations of headers, light boxes, product display areas, and cabinets. To serve as an entrance, a two-story structure was built. This also contained conference rooms and a theater area.

Exhibitor: U S West Inc.
Producer: Exhibits Inc.
Designer: Good Show! Inc.

Invite your competitors to share your space at a trade show? Seems unlikely, but that's what U S West did at the 12th International Switching Symposium. The combined exhibit attracted increased traffic and made possible an opportunity for all involved to show off their own special advantages. This was because propinquity permitted the holding of the U S West ISDN trials. ISDN stands for the Integrated Services Digital Network, a revolutionary technology which allows for the simultaneous transmission of voice, data and video over a single telephone line. This involved four different switch manufacturers, five terminal equipment suppliers and six users.

GIANT EXHIBITS

138　GIANT EXHIBITS

Exhibitor:	U S West Inc.
Producer:	Exhibits Inc.
Designer:	Good Show! Inc.

Invite your competitors to share your space at a trade show? Seems unlikely, but that's what U S West did at the 12th International Switching Symposium. The combined exhibit attracted increased traffic and made possible an opportunity for all involved to show off their own special advantages. This was because propinquity permitted the holding of the U S West ISDN trials. ISDN stands for the Integrated Services Digital Network, a revolutionary technology which allows for the simultaneous transmission of voice, data and video over a single telephone line. This involved four different switch manufacturers, five terminal equipment suppliers and six users.

Exhibitor:	Honda
Producer:	George P. Johnson Co.
Designer:	Doug Johnson

An architectural design philosophy was applied in the development of this exhibition to provide Honda with an image of strength and stability. The clean and simple lines reinforce the practical and functional aspects of Honda's marketing strategy. The deep blue and beige color scheme, complemented with subtle recessed brass accents, was chosen for its timeless elegance and attention to detail. Bold illuminated identification is incorporated into all platforms, and low product signage identifies each vehicle. All product information and color and trim displays were designed at a low height to avoid visual obstruction and to promote interaction on a personal level.

Exhibitor:	Caterpillar
Producers:	Exponents Inc; George P. Johnson Co.
Designer:	Disney Imagineering; George P. Johnson Co.

At 100,000 square feet, this is believed to be the largest exhibit ever created with a modular system. A key objective was a design that would not be dwarfed by the massive industrial machinery that would be on display. Strong corporate identity was achieved through the color scheme of yellow headers and colored dots. The exhibit included over 50 pieces of equipment, 25-foot high scenic murals, hi-tech fountains that shot jets of leaping water from one fountain to another, an enclosed theater, and three large structures. Designed for a show held once every six years, the components are now used for regular national and regional trade shows.

Exhibitor: Black & Decker (US) Inc.
Producer: Cyclonics Inc.
Designer: Martin Spicuzza

This 160′ × 40′ two-story exhibit had a superstructure built entirely of fiberglass structural shapes, including flat sheet, channels, angles, square tube and wide flange beams, some spanning 26-feet. It offered extensive slat-wall product display space, large graphics, and a full double deck for private conference areas.

GIANT EXHIBITS 143

Exhibitor:	Millipore Corp., Waters Chromatography Division
Producer:	Fahey Exhibits
Designer:	Dennis Healey

The main design objective was to create an open, walk-through atmosphere with flexibility in product and graphic displays. The use of Corian, a state-of-the-art material, created a clean, laboratory feeling. Product lines from different company segments could be displayed while sustaining a strong corporate identity.

Exhibitor:	Thomson CGR
Producer:	Fahey Exhibits
Designer:	Jeff Masters

This complex structure includes a self-supporting glass atrium and a full computer floor with air-conditioned computer rooms.

CHAPTER 6
Special Areas

The basis of marketing through trade shows is the opportunity for one-to-one contact. That is why product demonstrations, conference rooms, and theaters are often used as part of exhibits. They offer a special quality that no other marketing technique can match. This chapter looks at some of the ways in which designers have handled this special exhibition tool.

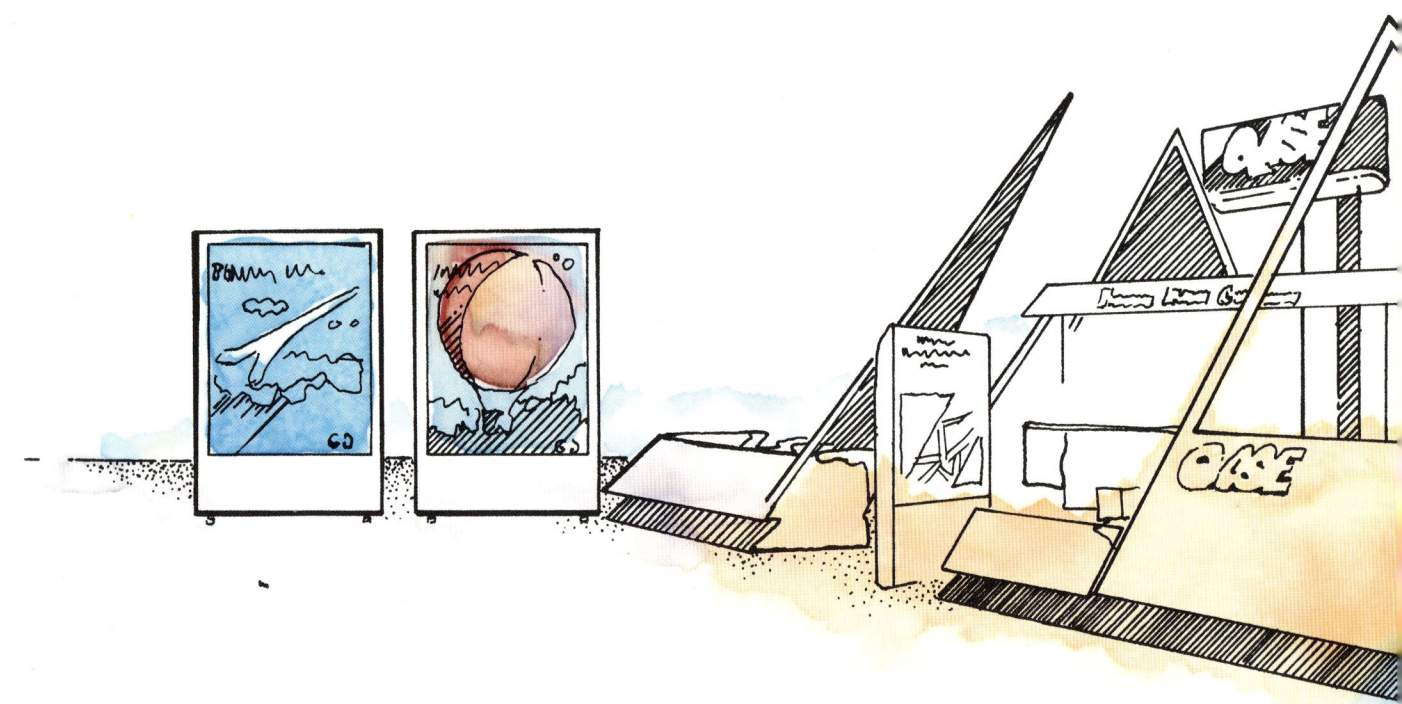

Exhibitor: British Airways
Producer/Designer: Nimlock Company

This lightweight, portable display offers a simple, large background for a presentation or demonstration. Weighing only 15 pounds, it can travel as baggage, and can be set up in moments without tools. The absence of a frame makes the 80 square foot mural seem even larger.

Exhibitor: Toro—Home Improvement Division
Producer: Heritage Display Group, St. Paul
Designer: Lee Randall

Use of the open mesh structure provides a maximum degree of openness and flexibility in merchandising. The strong horizontal black bases and headers control and define the space. A small conference area is included in the back of the booth.

Exhibitor: Bytheway's Manufacturing Inc.
Producer/Designer: 360 Designers & Producers

In this unusual demonstration technique, the window blinds were mounted between pillars. As each blind was opened, it revealed a large photo of a market place scene, demonstrating light control. The columns were made of PVC irrigation pipe, with automotive paints applied by hand.

Exhibitor: Huebsch Originators
Producer/Designer: Hartwig Exhibitors

Semi-private conference areas are shielded by railing-height partitions of smoked plastic.

SPECIAL AREAS 149

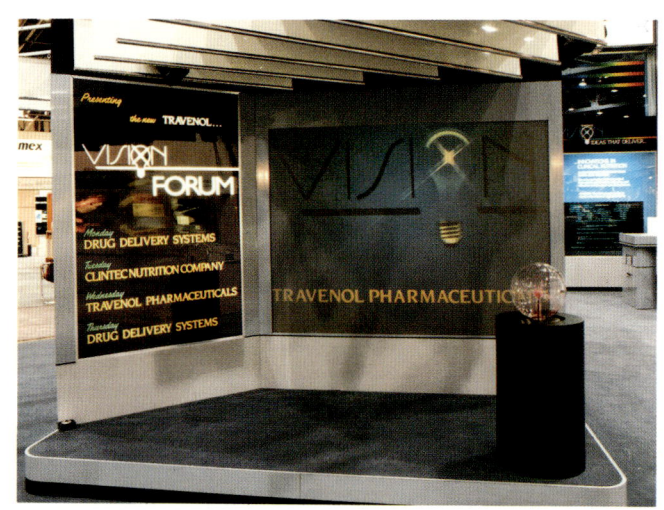

Exhibitor: Travenol
Producer: The Design Agency Inc.
Designer: Jacques Laliberte

Four divisions were included in this exhibit, and because of the openness of the design, they were always visually connected. A small stage served as the site for important presentations.

Exhibitor: The Gorman Rupp Company
Producer: Cyclonics Inc.
Designer: Martin Spicuzza

At both ends of this exhibit are demonstrations of pumps at work. The water movement adds to the excitement of the display. The modules under the deck are used in smaller groupings at smaller shows.

Exhibitor: Cardiac Pacemaker Inc.
Producer: Haas Display Co.
Designer: Dick Giffin

A hi-tech plasma discharge unit, specially adapted for this purpose, reacted with a large animated EKG demonstration to explain a product reaction to the heart's malfunctioning.

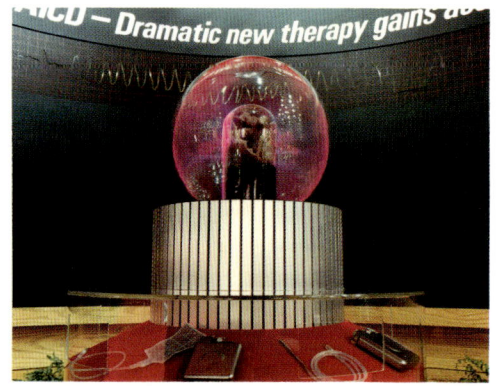

Exhibitor: Rampart Packaging
Producer: Beyond Exhibits Inc.
Designer: Teddie Jo Ryan

Using Exponents components, there is a comfortable conference room, and a working piece of equipment along the aisle edge of the space. The large graphic in the tower was duplicated on a billboard outside the hall.

Exhibitor: Campbell's
Producer: Geron Associates Ltd.
Designer: Ramon Brioux

An exhibit designed specifically for the distribution of food samples has strong company identification, but easily-interchanged product line identification.

Exhibitor:	Agfa Gevaert Inc.
Producer:	Structural Display Inc.
Designer:	Philip De Carolis

The cantilevered pylons, an unusual tradeshow structure, attracted attention though its strength and feeling of motion. The triangular pieces continued this feeling while its tunneling effect drew people into the booth.

Exhibitor: Sterling Plastics
Producer: Exhibit by Design
Designer: Jeff Burke

In a small island space, this centered booth was able to feature a new products section and a small conference area, and still leave plenty of room for display of the regular product line.

Exhibitor: Compugraphic Corp.
Producer: Display Workshop Inc.
Designer: Skip Day

A demonstration theater is outlined by a row of pillars set in a semi-circle. Slots in the base and top permit easy change from one configuration to another.

Exhibitor: CheckRobot
Producer: Fahey Exhibits
Designer: Paul Occhipinti

Introducing a self check-out counter for supermarkets, this was the exhibitor's first participation in a trade show. Three operating units were featured on a raised platform, with a truss ceiling over the demonstration offering light control and high visibility.

Exhibitor:	DuPont Company/Permacep Products
Producer:	Display Arts Studios
Designer:	Robert D. Mass

In an effort to make the small 10′ × 20′ booth look bigger, and still stay within basic show rules, curved walls were employed. The long wall on the left, with its wrap-around rails, provides privacy to the conference area.

Exhibitor: DuPont
Producer: Art Guild Inc.
Designer: Van Sickle & Rolleri

A fully-equipped demonstration area is at the back of the booth, while other hands-on demonstrations can be given to individuals elsewhere within the space.

Exhibitor: BWD Automotive
Producer: Exhibit by Design
Designer: Jeffrey Burke

The brand name products get more prominence in the signing than the parent company. The raised conference deck adds interest. Below the deck is storage space, accessed from inside a storage room.

Exhibitor:	Pier 1 Imports
Producer:	Freeman Design Display
Designer:	Rick Gronenfeld

A fiber optic map is the visual attraction in this simple booth which contains two conference areas.

Exhibitor: Amtrol
Producer: Las Vegas Convention Productions
Designer: Guy Petty

Natural wood and plenty of greenery provided a pleasing backdrop for the products on display. The changes in level also added interest.

Exhibitor:	NeoRx
Producer:	Giltspur Exhibits, Chicago
Designer:	Peter Brandt

An interesting approach to seating before video monitors with remote speakers is used here. Note the dark plexiglass area.

Exhibitor:	Four Seasons Hotel Corporation
Producer:	Freeman Design Display
Designer:	Jon Gunderson

Made to look like an elegant Four Seasons lobby, this exhibit houses a computer-controlled multi-image slide presentation.

Exhibitor: Knouse Foods
Producer: Dimension Works Inc.
Designer: Fred Svetlik

At one end of this peninsula booth runs a counter used for sampling the food products. At the other end are two conference rooms, set off by smoked plexiglass-topped rails. The wide open passage through the booth encouraged cross-traffic between two large displays of product.

Exhibitor: Pictel Corporation (now PictureTel)
Producer: Heritage Communications of St. Louis
Designer: Joe Hennessy

Teleconferencing procedures were demonstrated with three free-standing booths, one in each of three corners. A video of the demonstration was built into the tower of the fourth corner.

Exhibitor: Lederle Laboratories
Producer: ECOFA
Designer: Ralph Holker

Glossy vinyl-clad columns and giant lightboxes make this exhibit a crowd-stopper. The floating lightboxes provide privacy in two small conversation areas in the 20 × 30-foot island. The tall central column provides strong corporate identification and ample storage space.

Special Areas 165

Exhibitor: Lasag International
Producer: Exhibitgroup, Chicago
Designer: Ron Ferguson

Every inch of this 20' × 20' island is utilized. Included are two equipment demonstration areas, one mini-conference area, and an audio-visual area.

EXHIBITOR: Champion Spark Plug Company
PRODUCER/DESIGNER: Good Displays, Inc. (Toledo, Ohio)

With 21 products divided into three categories, to be introduced at this show, one product was selected from each category, and spotlighted in a larger-than-life model on a turntable. The truck at the dock was used as the stage for a performance that included unloading the new product and explaining its features and benefits.

Exhibitor: AT&T
Producer: Heritage Communications of St. Louis
Designer: Joe Hennessy

To demonstrate its products, AT&T turned its exhibit space into a working office. The cross-aisle spaces were tied together by transforming the aisle into a street, with street markings and working traffic lights.

Exhibitor: Acro Extrusion Co.
Producer: Display Arts Studios
Designer: Barbara A. Riggio

To achieve maximum product display, the product itself was used as part of the booth structure. The central tower helps to set off a semi-private conference area, and gives prominence to the company name.

Exhibitor: Hilti Inc.
Producer: Custom Exhibits Corp.
Designers: Hilti; Custom Exhibits

In order to catch the interest of the passerby, several kinds of motion were introduced. Rotating turntables were placed under the two neon signs on the back wall, an electronic messageboard, a rotographic display, and a video unit out front. The central counter was used to demonstrate the Hilti tools.

SPECIAL AREAS 169

Exhibitor: Pfahnstiehl Corporation
Producer/Designer: The Derse Company

Scattered tables with comfortable chairs permit a number of small conference settings, while for more privacy, there is the circular space on the central tower, just 4 feet above the hall floor. The component panels which carry much product, can be used in serpentine or free-standing set-ups.

Exhibitor: Tellabs
Producer: Giltspur Exhibits, Chicago
Designer: Peter Brandt

Overhead structures convey a networking image and serve the practical purpose of carrying wiring. The tower in one corner shelters a small conference area.

SPECIAL AREAS 171

Exhibitor: Olin Hunt
Producer: Intro Displays
Designer: Roger Ting

Four free-standing displays, each capable of standing alone as a 20-foot back wall, provide a hi-tech setting for photographic chemicals. Large flags suspended from the ceiling and a three-dimensional logo provide strong corporate identity.

Exhibitor:	Silicon Valley Group
Producer:	Dimensional Decor & Design Inc.
Designer:	Gayle Bryan

Two large pieces of equipment had to be demonstrated in a 10' × 20' area, which also had to contain some conference area. For protective reasons, one of the machines was placed in a quasi clean room, the other in an enclosed case. The small conference area was partially protected by a side wall and aisle railing.

Exhibitor: Rowenta
Producer: Dimension Works Inc.
Designer: John Wilen

A Meroform space frame provides the structural support for the cantilevered overhead aluminum pods. This allows an uninterrupted view of the product display and demonstrations. A conference area is in the rear center.

174 SPECIAL AREAS

Exhibitor: Abbott Laboratories
Producer: Impact Exhibits
Designer: Frank D. Nave;
Michael Eosbenner

Abbott wanted to call attention to itself as it entered the cardiovascular field. The three rows of lights above the semi-enclosed conference area symbolized the flow of blood, with the blue lights moving to the left, the magenta ones to the right, and finally, the red ones to the left. Large 35-inch monitors created an animated logo which turned into a brief introduction that led visitors to the interactive modules.

Special Areas 175

CHAPTER 7

Multi-Level

If the exhibit industry has an endangered species, it is the double-deck structure. At the time of writing, in the Fall of 1987, there are a number of actions being taken that may rule out, to all practical purposes, this particular classification of design.

The double-decker came into use when exhibitors at a sold-out show wanted more space and the only way they could get it was to move into an upper level. There are other advantages, however, to putting some functions above others. Conference and meetings rooms are quieter and less open to unwanted interruption when they are 8' × 10' above the working show floor. The compactness produced by having layers of exhibit means it is easier to get from one part to any other. The larger structure also is more imposing and perhaps more memorable.

The future of the double-deck, therefore, is unpredictable, but there are many in existence. This chapter illustrates a few.

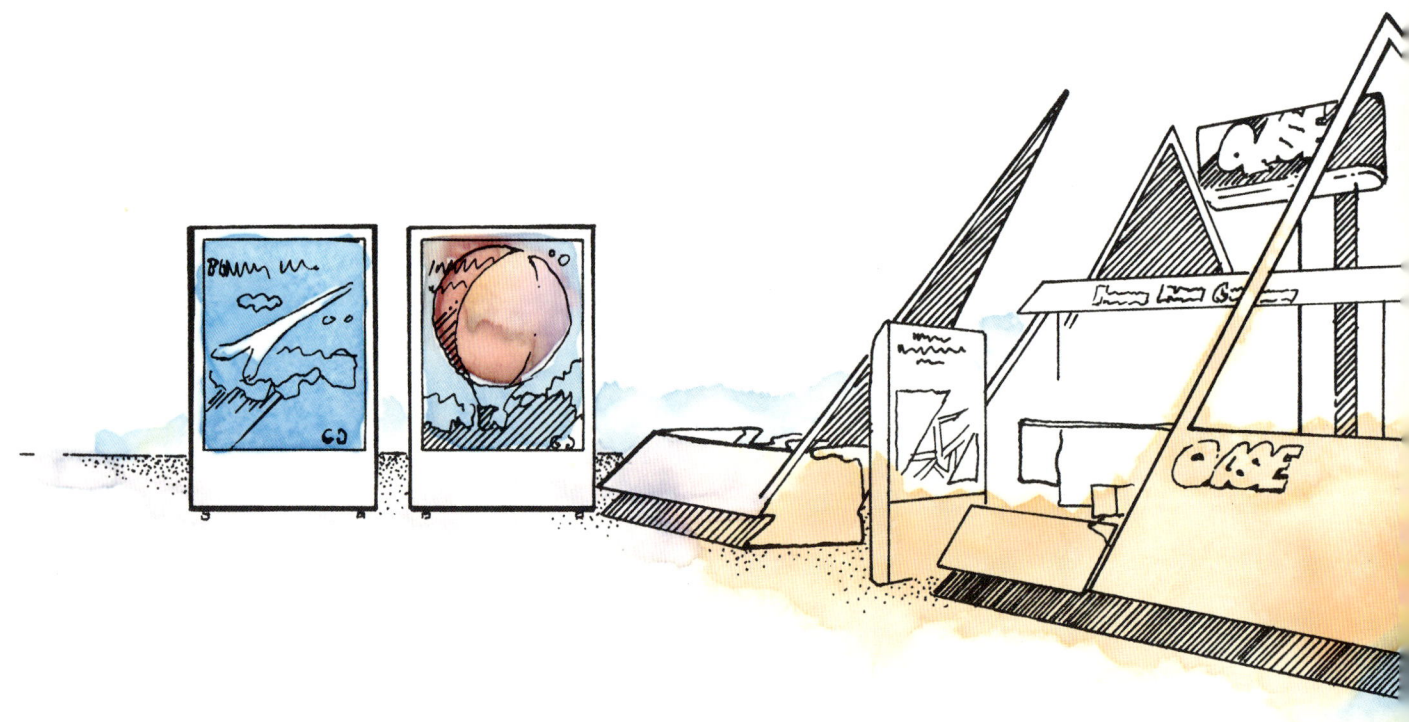

Exhibitor: General Foods
Producer: Exhibits Inc.
Designer: Neal Hoffman-Dana

The exhibitor's new logo was given prominence at both ends of the space, as well as from the walls of the large second-deck conference room. The kinetic light sculpture in the center of the sampling area attracted attention.

Exhibitor: Oster
Producer: Exhibitgroup, Chicago
Designer: Rick Lewis

When this exhibit was designed in 1985, it was 50 feet, but planned for future expansion, using a mirror image of the structure. The upper deck runs a full 100 feet.

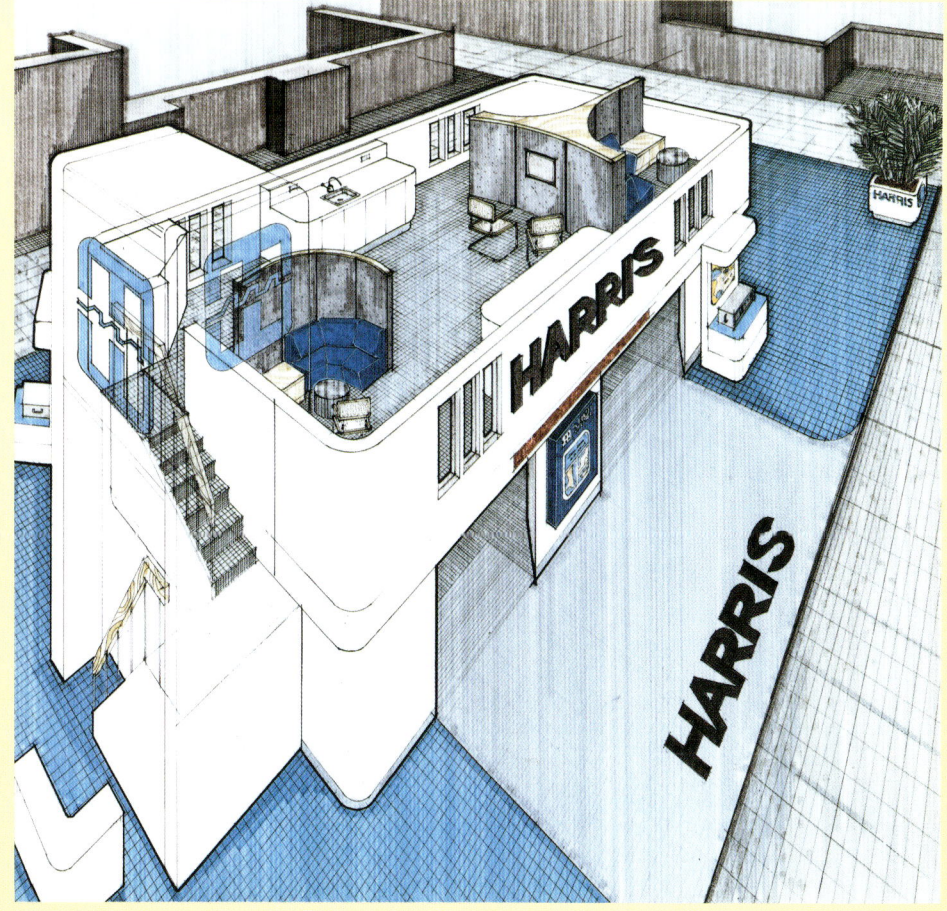

Exhibitor:	Harris Corporation
Producer:	Production House Inc.
Designer:	Design Plus Two Inc.

The central two-level structure holds three small conference areas, plus a viewing area for a video monitor. The free-standing units on the ground level use large graphics to explain the equipment.

Exhibitor:	Emhart
Producer:	Geron Associates Ltd
Designer:	Stuart King

This 70 × 10-foot two-level exhibit can be rearranged in a wide variety of configurations. The smoked plexiglass walls of the conference area give privacy without a hemmed-in feeling. Note how the slat-wall pattern is continued on the information desks and the columns.

Exhibitor:	Master Lock/Dexter Lock
Producer/Designer:	Hartwig Exhibitions Inc.

Eight double-sided modules carry easily-changed product displays. The second deck straddles two units, and can be omitted if there are height limitations.

Exhibitor: Hamilton Beach Inc.
Producer/Designer: Hartwig Exhibitions Inc.

A large number of product display modules surround an accessible demonstration desk. The large upper deck has room for conferences and a private office.

Exhibitor:	H. Altice Marketing
Producer:	Display Arts Studios Inc.
Designer:	Robert D. Mass

Each slat-wall alcove is used as a semi-private conference area. The superstructure, supported by a space frame, is now decorative only. To change it to a second-level conference area, a structural framework will be installed. A spiral staircase will be installed in a central storage closet.

Exhibitor: Hilton Hotel Corporation
Producer: Freeman Design Display
Designer: Tom Yurkin

Elegance is protrayed by these curved stairways with their brass railings.

MULTI-LEVEL 183

Exhibitor: American Electric
Producer: Cyclonics Inc.
Designers: Martin Spicuzza; Gina Roberts

To give the structure an architectural feeling, the superstructure was made of Extren fiberglas.

Exhibitor: Maxell
Producer: Exhibitgroup, NY
Designer: Richard Hassa

While many of the product displays are semi-enclosed, the display is open to the aisles. All conference rooms are on the second level.

Exhibitor: Canadair
Producer: Kadoke Display Ltd.
Designer: EAS Exhibition Services

A full sized cockpit and tail of an airplane calls attention to this display, while a round Octanorm doublefloor construction is used to build a VIP reception area in this striking display.

Exhibitor:	Anchor Food Service
Producer:	Dimension Works Inc.
Designer:	John Wilen

This 22 × 80-foot island was designed as three independent structures, which can be used independently in smaller spaces. The center unit incorporates four second-floor conference rooms.

Exhibitor: Display Systems Group
Producer: Display Service Co.
Designer: Paul Mon

Designed to demonstrate the Alusett system to exhibit builders, this fully-certified pre-engineered structure has unlimited installation life. Two forms of exterior cladding are included.

Exhibitor: Miles Pharmaceuticals
Producer: Charles Maltbie Associates
Designer: Joe Viamonte

The space included an interactive learning center and a theater on the ground level, and two separate conference areas on the second floor.

Exhibitor: Reynolds - Reynolds
Producer: Exhibitgroup, Cincinnati
Designer: David Diedrich

Large block graphics and plenty of demonstration stations help to position the exhibitor as an industry leader in computer systems designed for the automotive industry. The upper deck areas were used for product demonstrations and closing sales.

Exhibitor: Scitex American Corp.
Producer: Display Workshop Inc.
Designer: Skip Day

Here the upper level is supported on a space frame which suggests the exhibitor's logo.

Exhibitor: Edison/Cooper Lighting Group
Producer/Designer: Hartwig Exhibitions Inc.

This exhibit gets a remarkably large upper level in a small space. The display modules allow easy product renewal.

Exhibitor: Mobil
Producer: Giltspur Exhibits, Rochester
Designer: Thomas G. MacAllister

With a wide variety of products to be shown, this exhibit needed a clean, consistent look to hold it together.

Exhibitor:	Olympic/Lucite
Producer:	Exhibit Design Consultants Inc.; All West Display
Designers:	Joe Maricich; Craig Wollen; Tony Reynolds

Here's a solution to the challenge of fitting three private conference rooms, 2 semi-private conference areas, and a major new product demonstration in a 20′ × 30′ space.

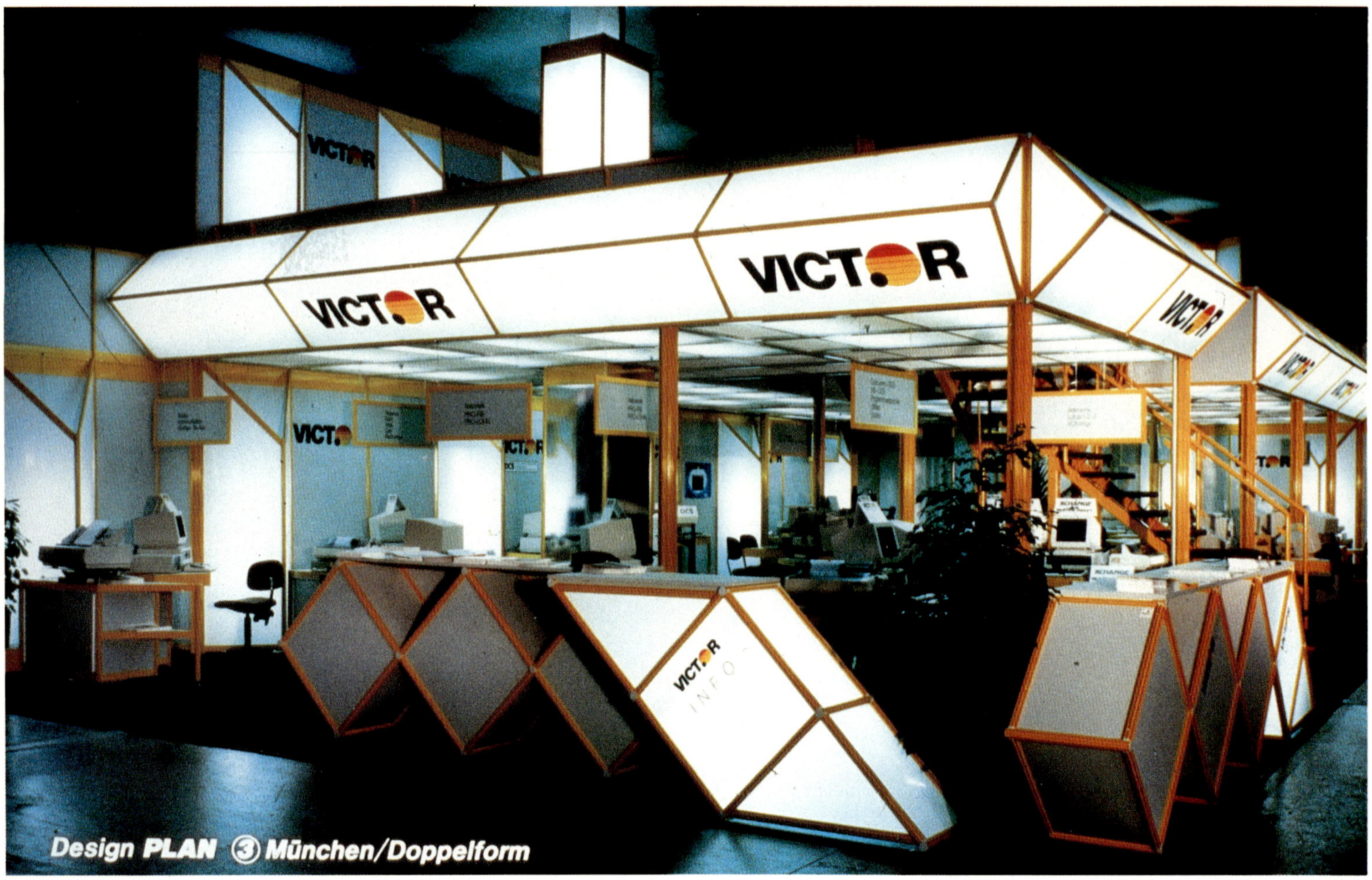

Exhibitor: Victor Computer
Producer/Designer: Plan 3

Illuminated fascias and display units highlighted both the company name and its new products. Using the modular Octanorm system, this exhibit can be used in several different configurations.

Exhibitor: Braun
Producer/Designer: Inform GmbH

This white powder-coated Octonorm structure offered the exhibitor a large conference area on the second floor, with a dramatic view of the entire exhibit hall.

Exhibitor:	Libbey St. Clair
Producer:	Exhibits International
Designer:	Paul Ciaraldi

A spiral staircase tucked between two semicircular alcoves for product display leads to a second-floor conference area, using less than 400 square feet of booth space.

MULTI-LEVEL 193

Exhibitor:	Texaco USA
Producer:	Exponents Inc; Giltspur Exhibits, Chicago
Designer:	Peter Brandt

This two-story structure demonstrates the merging of custom and modular exhibitry at its best. The Exponents system was used to dress the lower level, creating interest centers with large rear-illuminated transparencies, directing a smooth flow of traffic and enclosing an informal video viewing area. Giltspur created the mezzanine conference rooms and all structural supports.

Exhibitor:	Robert Bosch Power Tool Corp.
Producer/Designer:	Sugar Creek Studios Inc.

This space, 20' × 40', had to include displays of hundreds of tools, three demonstration areas using live equipment, as well as a conference area. Clear plexiglass was used around the demonstration areas as a safety precaution. The elements could also be used in an in-line configuration.

Exhibitor: Wilshire International
Producer: Cyclonics Inc.
Designer: Martin Spicuzza

A second level conference room was achieved in a structure that was only 20-feet wide and 10-feet deep. Product display was prominent on the floor level. Addition of more display panels could extend it to a 40-foot booth.

Exhibitor: Kohler
Producer: Heritage Display Group, Dallas
Designer: Mitch Gilbert

This massive structure seemed lighter because of its color and light graphics, offering a large display of product in a total environment.

MULTI-LEVEL 197

CHAPTER 8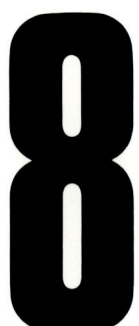

Showrooms and Offices

We think of exhibits as structures that are temporary, designed to last only the three or four days of a trade show, then to be dismantled, moved out, stored, and reinstalled at a later date in anther trade show. But the idea of working in three dimensions, of communicating or telling a story, can be applied in other realms, and exhibit designers are sometimes called to work along these lines. The examples shown in this chapter are of work utilizing trade show understanding, but whose end result is incorporated in an office or showroom.

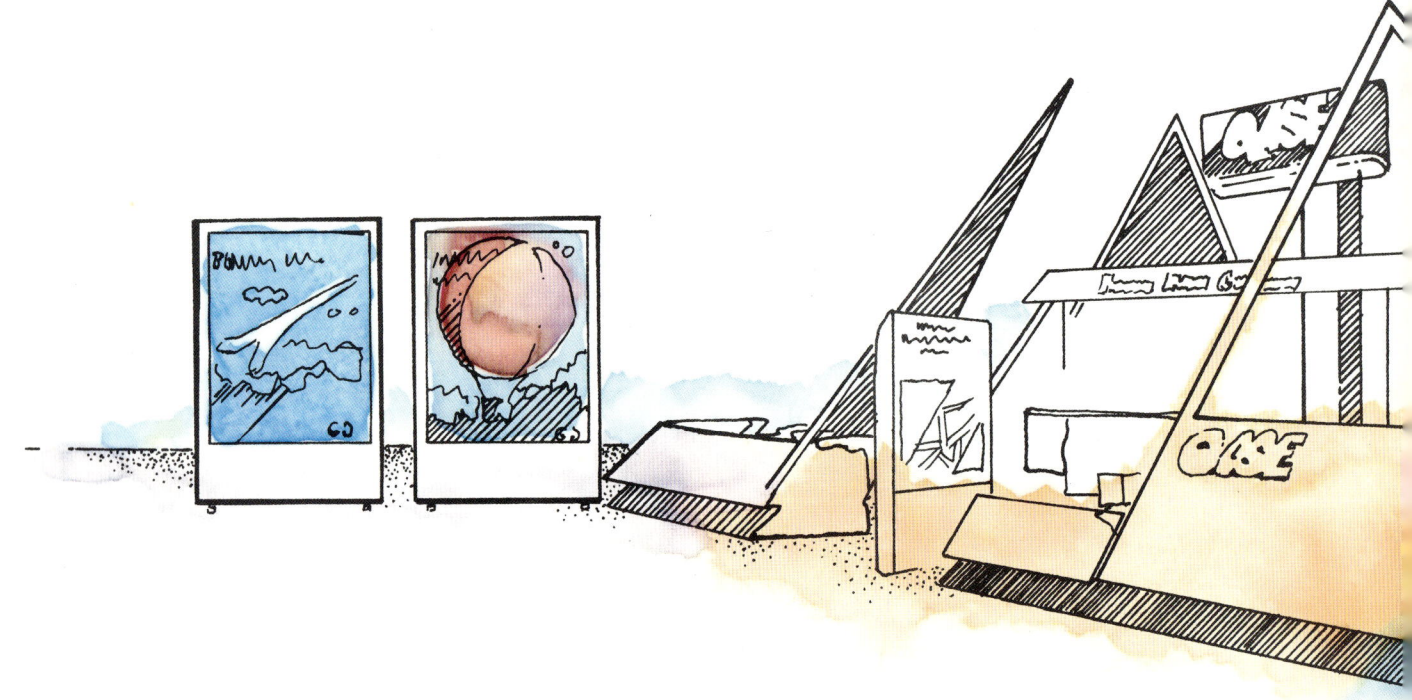

Exhibitor/Producer: T.L. Horton Design Inc.
Designer: Tony Horton

The clean, industrial look the company adopted for its own offices was designed so it would not compete with the scale models and photographs of the work it had done for its clients. All office materials are free-standing exhibit components.

SHOWROOMS & OFFICES 201

Exhibitor: AT&T Network Systems
Producer: George P. Johnson Co.
Designer: Robert Albitz; Alex Klimov

Highlighting the 13,000 square foot Showcase is a 5,000 square foot Product Demonstration Room, from which these pictures are taken. There are hands-on demonstrations of the Network System's products, enhanced by a modern audio-visual theater, elegant conference facilities complete with audio-visual capabilities, video teleconferencing, and an executive level hospitality facilty. The Showcase features complete top-to-bottom modularity. Everything from a major product demonstration and audio-visual presentation to the welcoming signs and luncheon menus can be adapted to a specific customer visit.

204 SHOWROOMS & OFFICES

Exhibitor: Coca Cola Foods
Producer: Custom Fixtures and Displays
Designer: Jeffrey Rafla

This dramatic showcase stands in the company headquarters lobby and presents its basic products. The items seem to float in the case, being well lighted from above and resting on a backlighted base and illuminated boxes of Corian.

Exhibitor: Wisconsin Electric Power Co.
Producer: The Derse Company
Designer: Maritz Communication Company

This spacious exhibit, in the lobby of corporate headquarters, encourages visitors to move about, and to use a wide variety of interactive elements that provide information.

206 SHOWROOMS & OFFICES

Exhibitor:	GTE
Producer:	Exhibitgroup, Cincinnati
Designer:	Earl Heintzelman

Located in the Dallas Infomart, this spectacular showroom is designed like a museum but also includes spaces for demonstrations and presentations to specific customer groups. Excitement starts from the corridor, with the brightly-lit logo beside the reception desk and the comfortable lounge area. Interactive exhibits can be used independently or be made part of a presentation by GTE personnel. They are far enough apart so that use of one by a group does not interfere with the use of another. Alcoves like this serve to display product groupings. An exciting presentation is given inside a simulated space capsule made of molded fiber. A view inside the "Connections" space capsule shows the large viewport through which passengers/visitors watch an exciting multi-media show during an imaginary space voyage. Other presentations can be given in the 75-seat, fully-equipped theater, which has its own impressive foyer. A number of small conference rooms are available for small group presentations. The walls of these alcoves can accept interchangeable copy/graphic panels tailored to the specific customer to whom a presentation is being made. Finally, a completely-enclosed conference room, also fully-equipped, is available when privacy is essential.

SHOWROOMS & OFFICES 207

Exhibitor:	Vail Associates
Producer:	Design Dynamics/Exhibits
Designer:	Roger M. Rios

The lobby of the executive offices of Vail Associates in Beaver Creek was designed to communicate real estate opportunities in Beaver Creek and the Vail Valley. A sense of the seasons and a reflection of Vail's unique architecture was brought indoors through prisms and display module design derived from European village gables.

Exhibitor:	Southern Bell
Producer:	Murphy & Orr Co.
Designer:	George W. Stough

A series of three-sided exhibits was designed for the lobby of the exhibitor's corporate headquarters. One side was a transparency grid representing a communications technology, with the two other sides housing interactive displays which explained how that technology could be put to use. The final display is a circular unit which discusses the future of telecommunications. Two video programs activated by motion detectors give the viewer insights into communications systems which will become available in the home and the office.

Exhibitor:	NCNB National Bank
Producer:	Pentes Design Inc.
Designers:	Lynn Holloway; Jack Pentes

This Christmas display was designed for a bank lobby with limited floor space but unlimited ceiling height. This triple-deck animated structure was an enlargement of a table-top version.

SHOWROOMS & OFFICES 209

CHAPTER 9
Museums

The museum exhibit is in a category of design all by itself. Its life span is considerably different, since it is expected to remain in position for a longer time than a trade show exhibit. It may be considered a permanent installation, which simply means that no date of dismantling and replacement has been set, or if it is a traveling exhibition, that it is destined to stay for limited periods in a limited number of locations. But like the trade show exhibit, it is a means of communication. Unlike the trade show exhibit, it stands by itself, with no staff to intervene between its story and its visitor.

Museum designers tend to concentrate on designing for museums, and while there are exceptions, those individuals and organizations that specialize in museum work do not usually have construction facilities. Because of the more-or-less permanent nature of these installations, new techniques of presentation often appear first in museum exhibits, and thus it is worth every designer's time to keep an eye on what is happening in this field of specialization.

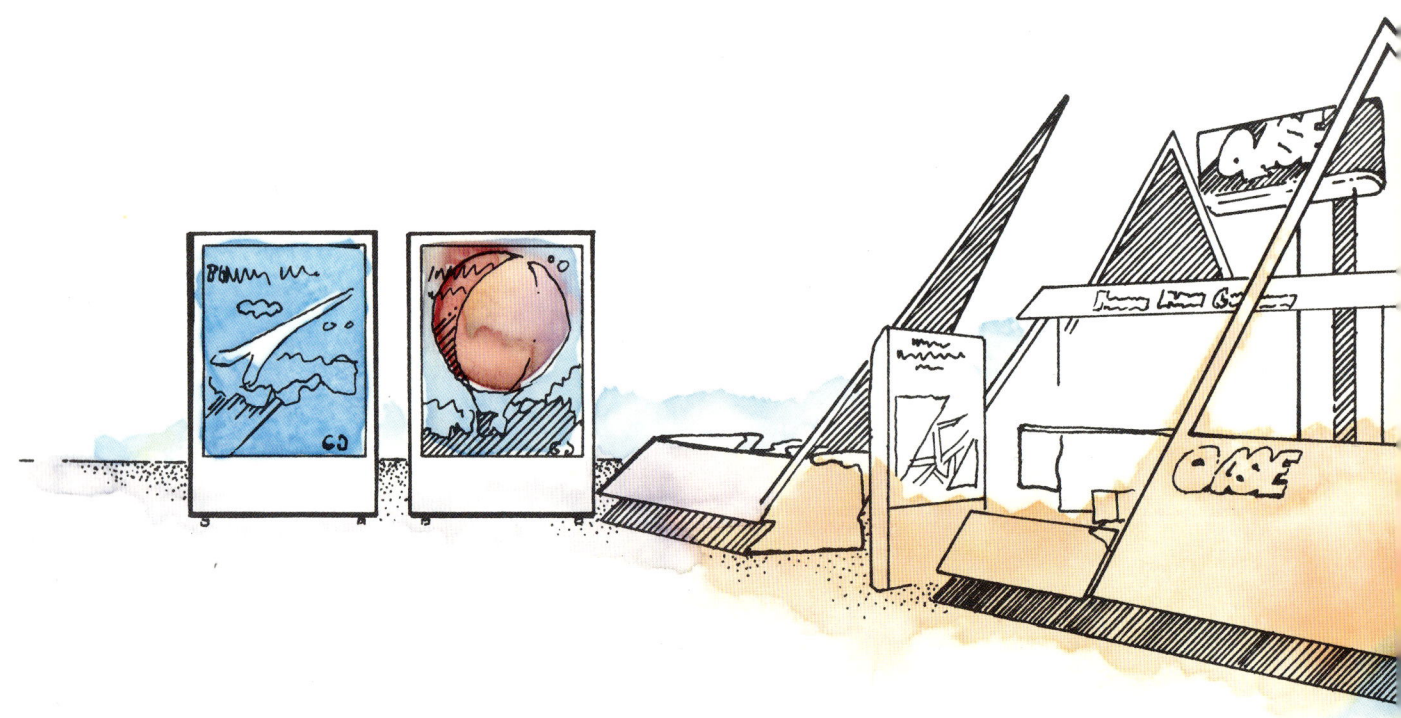

Exhibitor:	Georgia Institute of Technology; Republic of China
Producer:	Sugar Creek Studios Inc.
Designer:	Heery & Heery Architects; Sugar Creek Studios

The collection of Chinese artifacts toured the country, with each host museum designing and constructing its own display settings. Each of the eleven sections was entered through its own specially made portal which suggested both by legend and by design what lay ahead.

Exhibitor:	Father Flanagan's Boys Home
Producer:	Eisterhold/Llewellyn Exhibit Services
Designer:	Gerard Eisterhold

Life-size figures, used against realistic replicas, were extremely effective on an emotional level.

Exhibitor:	Anchorage Museum of History and Art
Producers:	Color & Design Inc; PML Exhibit Services Ltd
Designer:	Vincent Ciulla Design Associates Inc.

This exhibit was designed for a new extension of the museum, already under construction. A series of full-sized replicas of major dwelling types provided the focus for each chronological period of that exhibit. The dwellings are seen in section, with the furnished and inhabited interiors facing inside, to take full advantage of the natural light. Plenty of space is available in front of each dwelling to allow for large groups of students and tourists, the most frequent visitors to the museum. Benches double as boxes to hold items used by docents during demonstrations.

216 MUSEUMS

Exhibitor:	Block Island Historical Society
Producer:	P R Guest Inc.; Superior Phototech
Designer:	Vincent Ciulla Design Associates Inc.

This small scale exhibit showed how the people and their activities influenced the local architecture. With artifacts, photo blowups, a limited number of cases and platforms, and a video presentation, the exhibit shows how the farmers, fishermen, summer vacationers, and preservationists of Block Island each contributed to the whole.

Exhibitor:	DeWitt Wallace Decorative Arts Gallery, Colonial Williamsburg
Producer:	Design & Production
Designer:	Vincent Ciulla Design Associates Inc.

The design addresses three different levels of interest among the visitors to this outstanding collection of decorative items. The casual visitor can walk through the centrally-located Masterworks section of the gallery for an overview of the collection. Special interpretive exhibits are in the galleries on either side. The first such exhibition, for example, dealt with the interaction between the patron and the tradesman, and how the patron influenced the final product. The deeply interested visitor, probably a scholar or collector, can delve even further into the collection, with many study galleries.

Exhibitor:	First Tennessee Bank
Producer:	David C. Mancini
Designer:	Vincent Ciulla Design Associates Inc.

This traveling exhibit, "Tennessee Celebrates," was to visit five museums throughout the state, with space ranging from 5,000 to 7,000 square feet. To handle this variation, seven modules, each representing a theme, were prepared. Each incorporated popular materials associated with the subject, and contained a video monitor which ran a continuous program on the theme.

Exhibitor:	Pacific Science Center
Producers:	Pacific Science Center;
	W. Scott Robinson Designs Inc.
	Dinamation of California
Designer:	Daniel Quan Design

The exhibit centered on 10 different animated models of dinosaurs, half-sized but otherwise realistic. They were displayed in a bold theatrical manner in a large room which could be reached only by going through a dark, narrow cave. Each of the models was in its own alcove, a theatrical diorama. The platforms, of varying heights, also served the purpose of keeping visitors out of reach of the complex models without stanchions or ropes. The dinosaurs were supported by a group of interactive displays, including computer games, question and answer boards, touch fossils, graphics and a visitor-controlled dinosaur skeleton.

Exhibitor:	Pacific Science Center
Producers:	Pacific Science Center;
	Government of India
Designer:	Daniel Quan Design

An exhibit built and shown in India, of standard aluminum posts and panels, needed revision for exhibition in the United States. Starting with the concept of an Indian bazaar, the exhibit was organized around a marketplace defined by tent structures and colorful overhead banners. Around this central theme were narrow "streets" lined with exhibits and artisans practicing their crafts. The original aluminum system was retained, for the sake of economy, but was softened and partially obscured by the use of wood railing, plants, draped fabrics, and new signage and graphics. A new entrance, using a model of the Taj Mahal, acted as a transition space into the marketplace.

Exhibitor: St. Louis Science Center
Producer: Midwest/Backer Woodworks
Designers: Paul Maher; Paul Groenier

The Discovery Room is a place where children, three to twelve years old, may learn by doing. It covers nature, geology, culture, anatomy, and technology. A central area is designed for an introductory talk, after which visitors can experience the various exhibits.

Exhibitor: St. Louis Science Center
Producer: Advertisers Display & Exhibits Inc.
Designers: Paul Groenier; Jon Cournoyer

This exhibit on earthquakes includes seven interactive components, including a shake platform which allows visitors to feel what an earthquake is like. There are touch-screen computers and a seismometer which registers the passage of visitors through the gallery.

Exhibitor: Searle Pharmaceuticals Inc.
Producer/Designer: Sugar Creek Studios Inc.

Intended for eventual installation in a museum, this exhibit was first shown at an international medical meeting in Brazil. Its major element is a walk-through, anatomically correct model of the human stomach.

Exhibitor:	Waste Management Inc.
Producer:	Design Craftsmen
Designer:	Maritz Communications

The central core of this exhibit installed in Chicago's Museum of Science and Industry has a number of panels with audio-visual presentations in a housing that suggests modern industry. Alcoves around the outside of the space go into further detail on specific topics, with each simulating its environment, such as a landfill, an urban neighborhood, an industrial plant. A touch-screen computer game encourages visitors to make decisions and share their opinions on the subject of waste handling.

Exhibitor:	The German Marshall Fund of the United States
Producer:	Research & Design Associates
Designer:	Ann Catherine Fallen

This traveling exhibit explained how the Marshall Plan built cooperation in the rebuilding of Europe after World War II, using extensive black and white photography, mounted on panels built with Leitner elements.

Exhibitor:	Conoco Inc.
Producer:	McMillan Group
Designer:	Nancy and Charles McMillan

Entitled "Oceans of Promise," this traveling exhibit covered five areas of ocean use. In addition to flat, easy-to-ship panels, video footage was used to show new creatures found at extreme depths as well as new alternative energy and natural resources.

Exhibitor:	M/V City of St. Louis
Producer:	Heritage Communications
Designer:	PGAV Design Inc.

When a towboat was converted to a tourist attraction, an exhibit area was installed in a very small space on the second deck of the boat. The history of towboating was shown by using large photographs, accompanied by narrative, mounted on sheets of plexiglass suspended from the ceiling. Banners hanging between the clear panels added color to the exhibit.

Exhibitor:	The Christian Science Publishing Society
Producer:	McMillan Group with Scotia Woodworking
Designer:	Nancy and Charles McMillan

Designed to show visiting journalists the exhibitor's involvement in international news coverage, the exhibit is being expanded to become a multimedia visitors center on the presentation of news in newspapers, radio, shortwave and television. The tubular frames and truss work blend remarkably well with the arches and columns of the old building that houses the exhibit.

Exhibitor:	New York Public Library
Producer:	Exhibitgroup, New York
Designer:	Charles Froom

Designed to fit into an existing space, these 62 special vitrines displayed irreplaceable archival materials. Enclosed in plexiglass, these solid birch cases were equipped with battery-powered alarm devices, silica humidity-absorbing trays, invisible locking devices, diffused lighting, and fans/ventilation panels to maintain a constant dry air environment.

Exhibitor:	Monticello Visitors Center
Producer:	Charles Maltbie Associates
Designer:	Ralph Appelbaum Associates Inc.

This new visitor's center, outside Thomas Jefferson's home, looks at his life from various points of view. His architectural vision is represented in personal sketches and in new models of the original versions of the house, as well as of buildings that he planned for the estate but never executed. His application of science to agriculture is shown by a full-scale model of a plough he designed specifically for the Virginia country. And his attempts to make the plantation totally self-sufficient are show in his recordkeeping and in his meticulous analysis of the growing patterns of his crops. Two videotape productions show parts of the house not open to the public, and the glory of the gardens in full bloom.

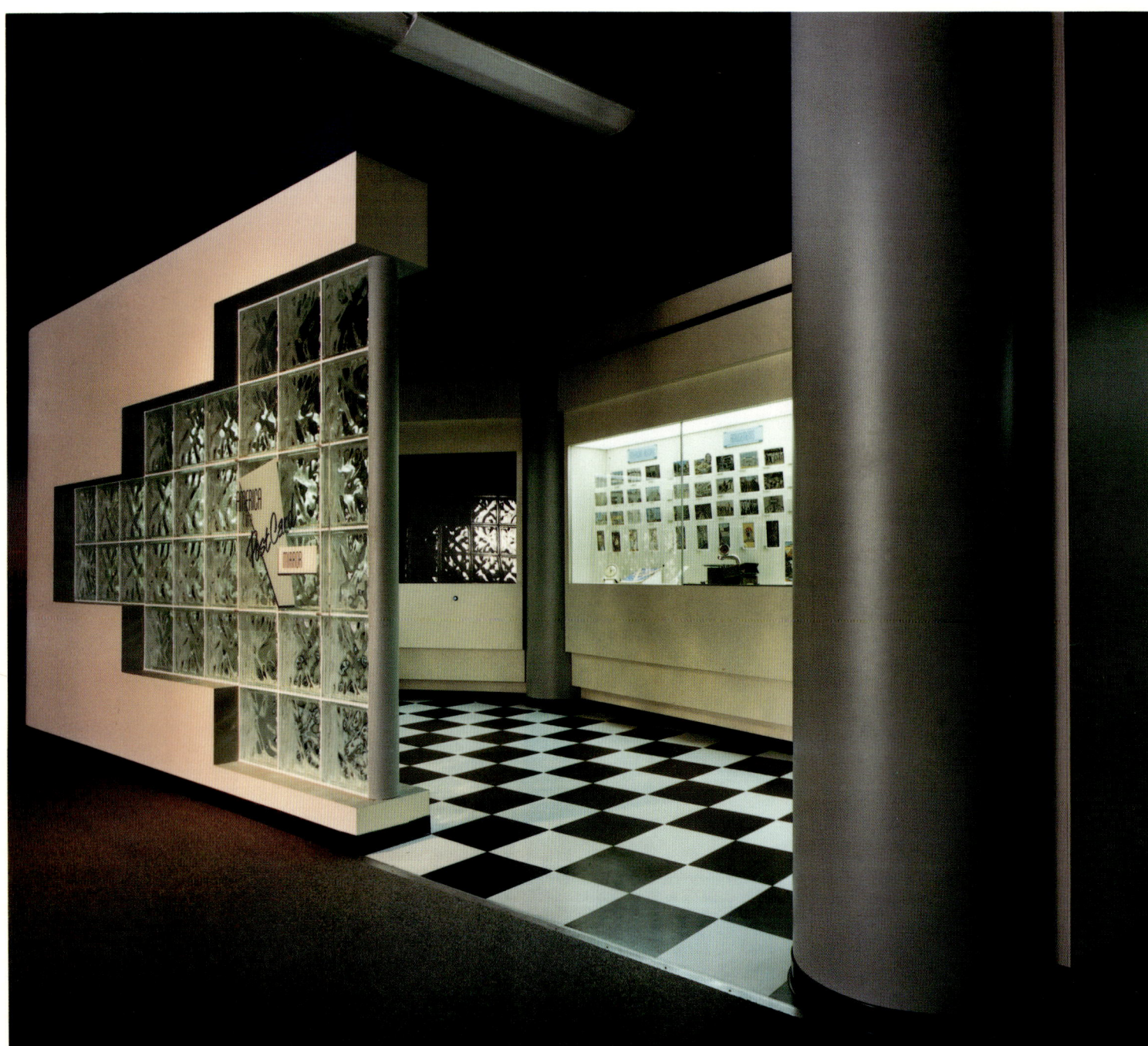

Exhibitor: Lake County Museums
Producer: Euro Domestic Exhibits
Designer: Maritz Dimensional Communications

Incorporating the deco style of the 1930s, this display of old postcards, accompanied by a slide show, takes a look back at the early 20th Century.

Exhibitor/Producer: Science Museums of Charlotte
Designer: Barry Echinger; Scott Chamberland

The use of Interlock snap trusses makes this exhibit easy to install and transport, and lends a hi-tech appearance.

Exhibitor: Jimmy Carter Presidential Museum
Producer: Click Systems Ltd.
Designer: Design & Production Inc.

The showcases, large and complex, were made from standard system parts, but built to exacting specifications to blend with the architectural finishes and features in the rest of the space.

Exhibitor: Texas and Southwestern Cattle Raisers Association
Producer: Exhibitgroup, New York
Designer: DeMartin, Marona Cranstoun and Downes

Using multimedia, visitors are helped to relive the trail drives that reshaped the cattle industry, learn about the pioneers who carved out ranches from this rough frontier, and discover the men and women who developed and made the cattle business into today's dynamic industry.

Exhibitor: Southern Bell
Producer: Murphy & Orr Company
Designer: George W. Stough

This compact museum, about 1700 square feet, charts the history of the telecommunications industry in America, with emphasis on Southern Bell's heritage. The displays revolve around a 1920s street scene, including a Model T repair truck and a lifesize lineman on a fully outfitted, multi-tiered pole. A mini-theater, that contains changing scenes and transmission display complete the story ending with an electronic question and answer world map that allows the viewer to compare telecommunications data from country to country.

CHAPTER 10
Some Interesting Ideas

In the course of preparing this book, many hundreds of entries, consisting of photographs and drawings supported by written descriptions, were sent to me for my consideration. For a variety of reasons, some of them were not suitable for any of the preceding eight chapters. The reasons for this were varied.

A number of them showed models and not the actual construction, and since I had, perhaps arbitrarily, decided that only photographs of completed projects would be used in those chapters, these models had to be ruled out.

But the design ideas were worth talking about and showing, so they were included in this chapter. Other entries showed only an interesting detail, and not the exhibit as a whole. Again, I felt the idea was too stimulating to be omitted, so here they are.

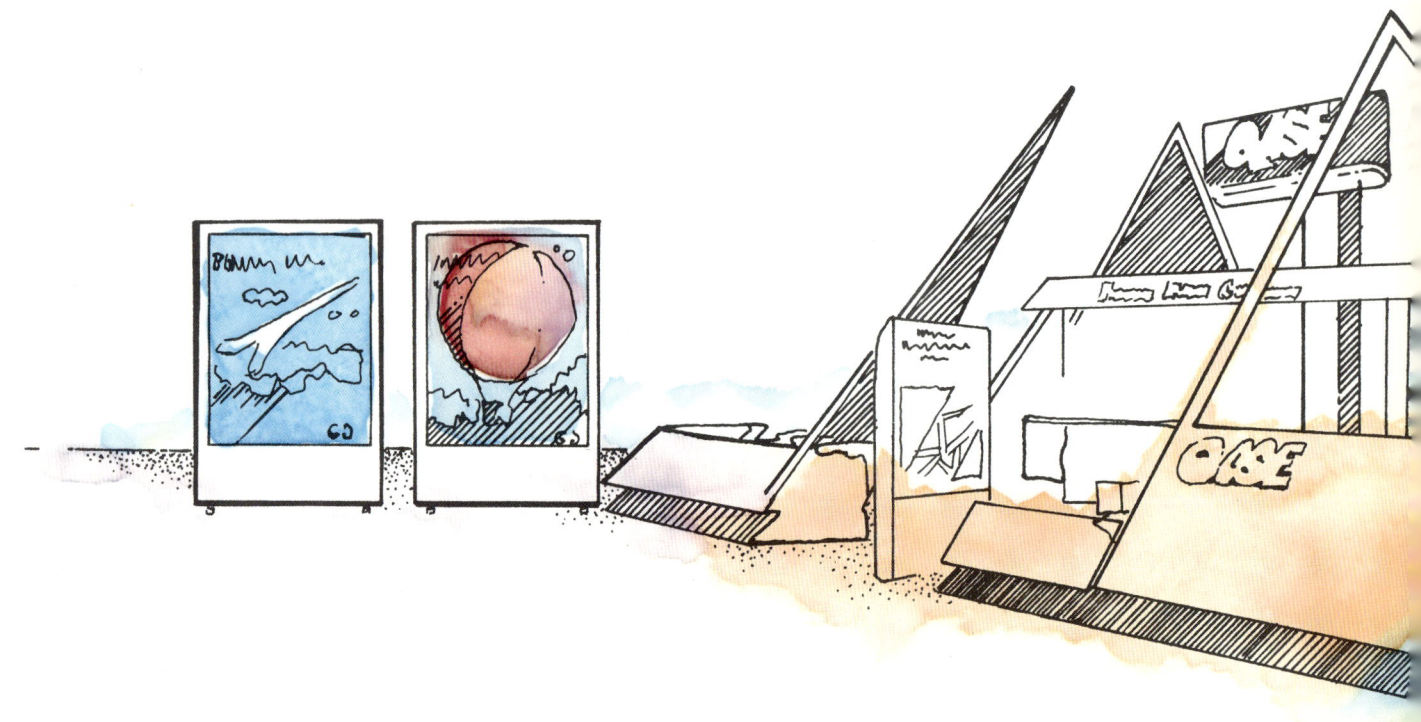

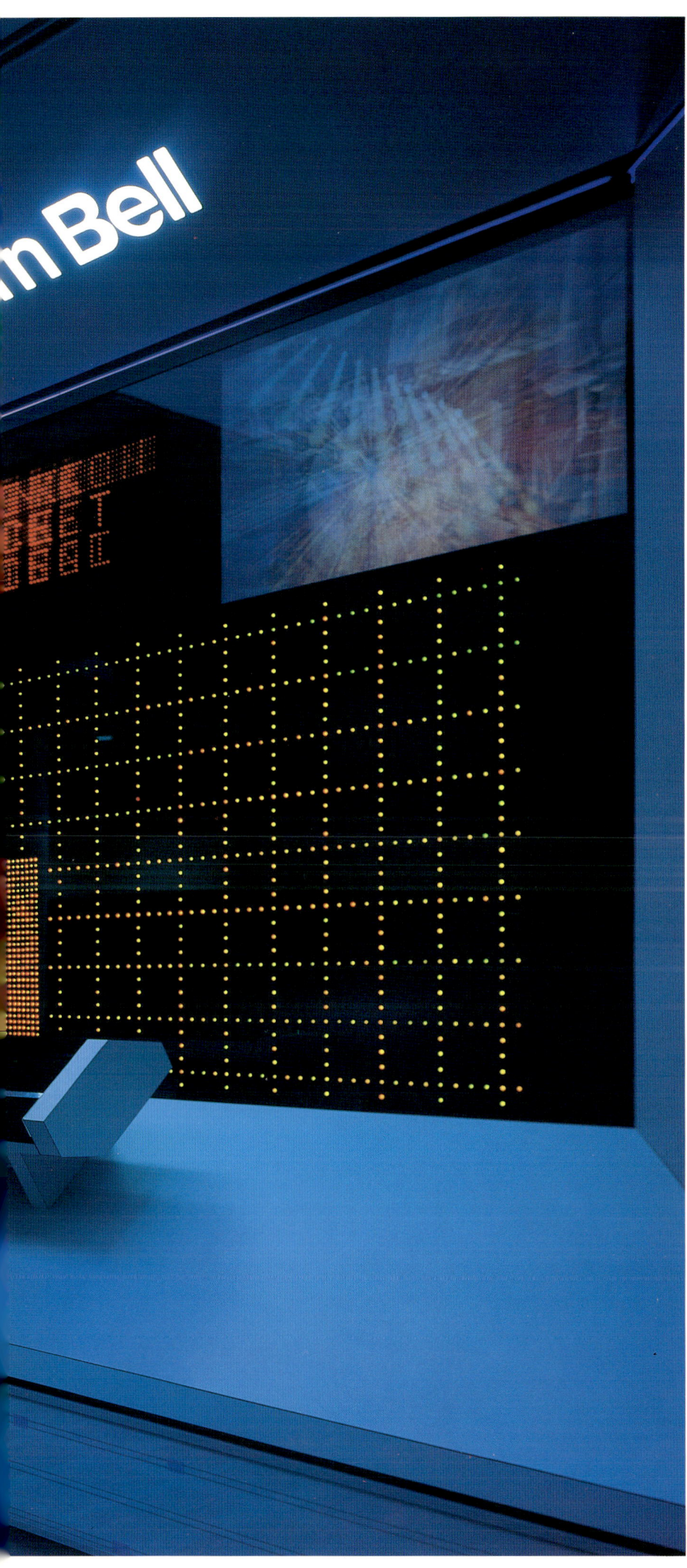

Exhibitor: Southern Bell
Producer: Murphy & Orr Co.
Designer: George W. Stough

This permanent installation in the Georgia World Congress Center uses, in one half, a 10-foot wide illustration on which are mounted a variety of modern equipment used or sold by the exhibitor. The other half represents its network services, using thousands of LEDs to form a matrix representing the network, augmented by a two-screen, four projector slide presentation.

Exhibitor:	Hazel/Cardinal/Josetens Business Products Division
Producer:	Haas Display
Designer:	Dick Giffin

A large amount of product can be displayed in this exhibit, shown here in model form. The elements can be rearranged as two across the aisle displays, and there is provision for a second-level space above the existing conference room.

Exhibitor:	NYNEX Corporation
Producer:	Denby Associates
Designers:	Kent Jones; Tony Lualdi

Designed for the company's annual stockholder's meeting, this stage set included a 40-foot expanse of block letters, which rose dramatically on a concealed elevator platform at the conclusion of a multi-projector, audio-visual show.

Exhibitor: JVC Company of America
Producer: Exhibitgroup Las Vegas
Designer: Shelton Adell

Here is a dramatic solution to the request for a way to display new products at trade shows, airports and shopping malls. The kiosk is equipped with a turntable, eight monitors and VCR's, and is capable of continuous audio and video presentations, with 360 degree product and presentation visibility.

SOME INTERESTING IDEAS 239

Exhibitor: Xerox Corporation
Producer: Giltspur Exhibits, Rochester
Designer: Mark Norenberg

Using Profile 100 system permitted the designer to develop a flexible, comparatively low-cost exhibit backwall, which included product counters. Vacuum-formed graphic panels permitted simple changes in appearance from market to market.

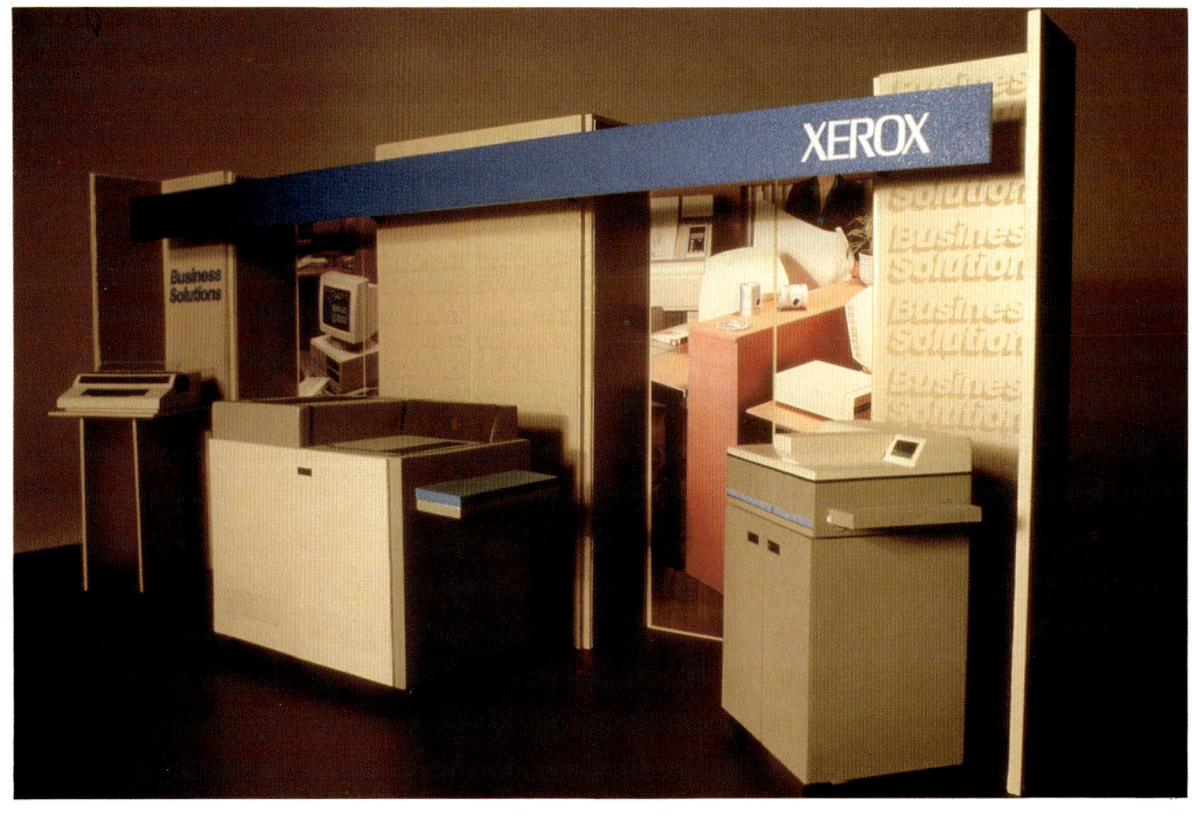

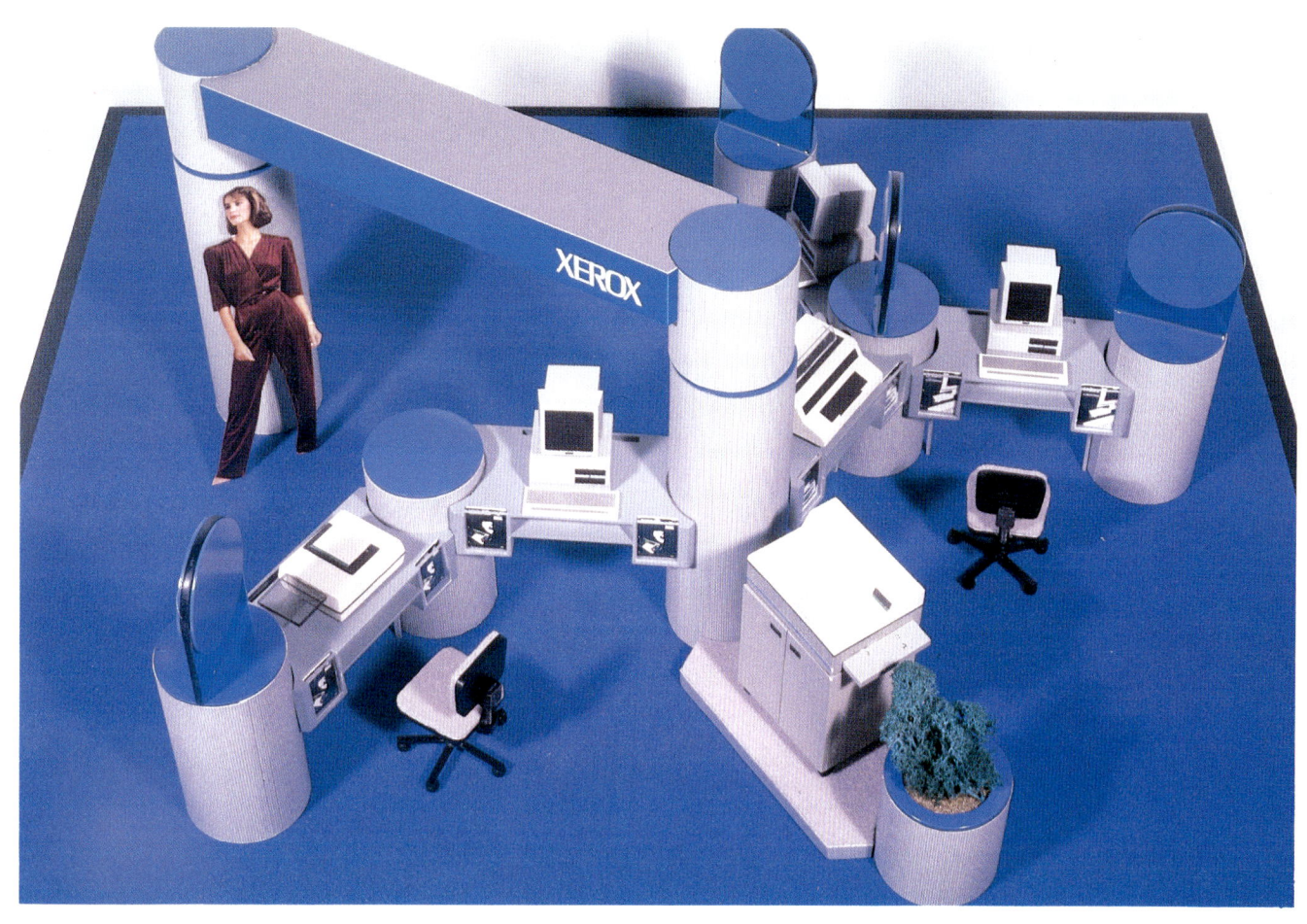

Exhibitor:	Fairchild Industries
Producer:	Giltspur Exhibits, Pittsburgh
Designer:	Isabelle Nardelli

The client needed two separate conference rooms, each for a different division, but needed to keep them under one umbrella. Note the interesting overhead treatment.

Exhibitor:	Sandoz Pharmaceuticals
Producer:	Intro Displays
Designer:	Roger Ting

Understated elegance and simplicity characterize this sponsored message and service center at a medical trade show. The exhibitor provides a central message board, along with general information about the meeting program and local facilities, as well as a list of its products for the medical meeting specialty.

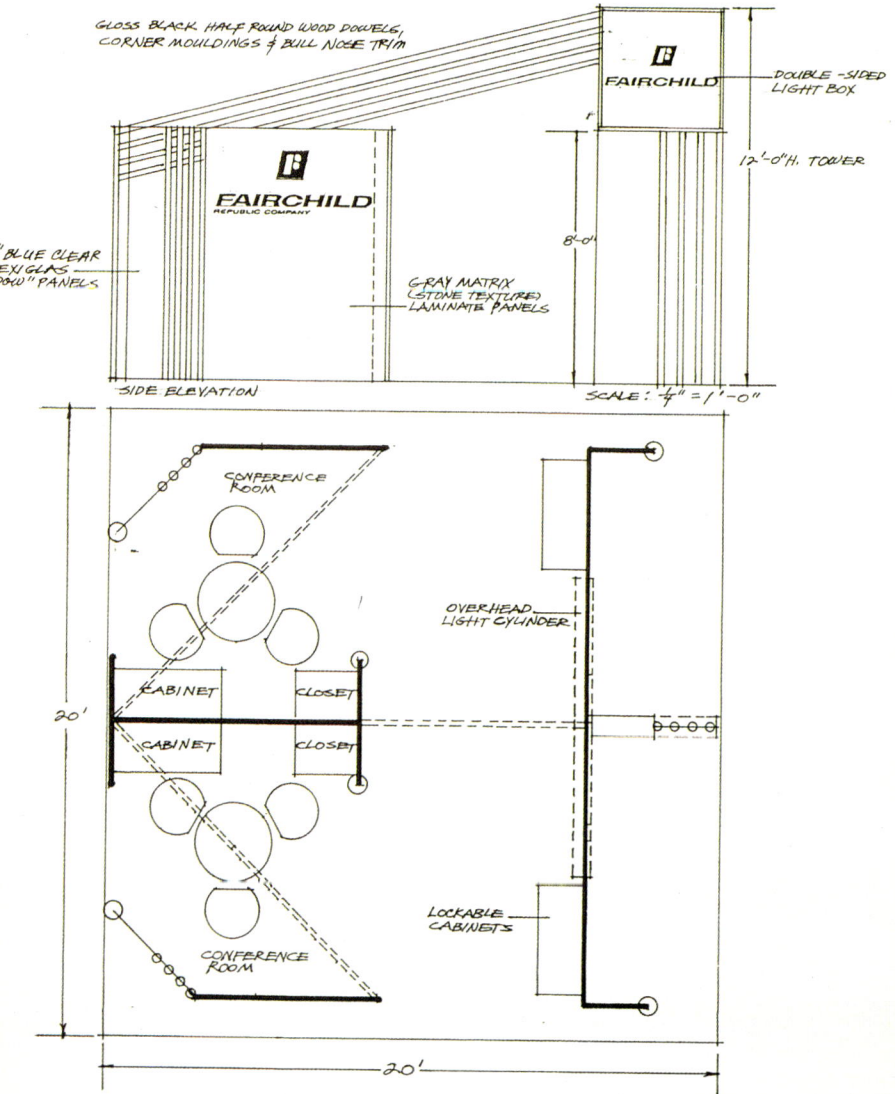

Some Interesting Ideas 243

Exhibitor:	Coast to Coast Hardware Stores
Producer/Designer:	United Longchamp International Inc.

For its private trade show, the exhibitor wanted a way of setting off a special area for presentations and other events, without occupying too much space or taking too much of the budget. This imaginative suggestion of a spaceship, built with Meroform elements and foamcore panels, was the solution. Special panels tied in with the show theme, "The Right Stuff."

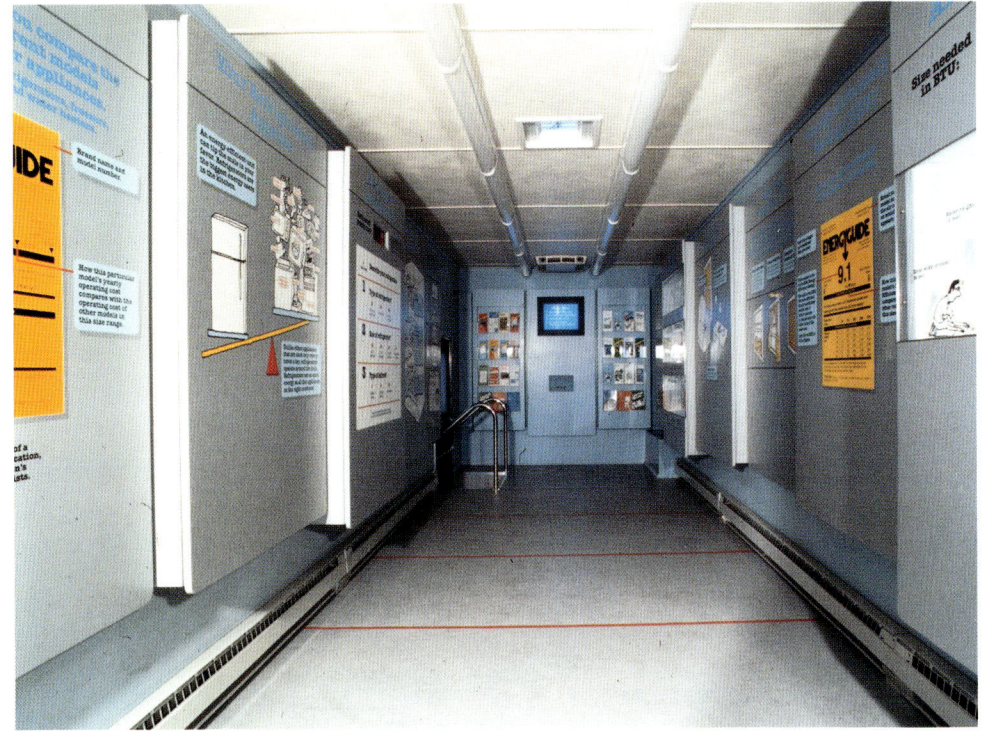

Exhibitor: Con Edison
Producer: Exhibitgroup, New York
Designer: Alex Karpilov

A converted RV became a traveling exhibit on energy conservation, illustrating how New Yorkers can economize on energy bills. Interactive displays, audience participation and animated graphics helped get its message across.

Exhibitor: AT&T
Producer: Exhibitgroup, New York
Designer: Jorge O. Sosa

This illuminated tunnel employs sequentially-flashing tubes to guide visitors from the third to the second level of an exhibit area. The lights in the 34 plexiglass arches go on sequentially from one end of the walkway to the other.

Exhibitor: USAir
Producer/Designer: Downing Displays Inc.

This portable display was designed to serve as a backdrop for USAir representatives during presentations around the country, so it had to be flexible, portable and easy to handle. The unit can be shipped by UPS, and can be set up and taken down in minutes without the use of tools.

Exhibitor: Metro-North Commuter Railroad
Producer: Syma Systems Inc.
Designer: John McKeon; Wayne Ehman

This outdoor information kiosk, made of stock exhibit elements, had to stand up to all weather conditions in a northern climate.

Exhibitor:	Electrocom Automation
Producer:	Heritage Display Group, Dallas
Designer:	Ken Konke

In order to bring the product to the customer, this motor home was customized. The interior accommodated high-tech equipment, offering the prospect an opportunity for hands-on experience with the product. Dynamic graphics reinforced the company image and logo.

Exhibitor:	Ford Motor Company
Producer:	Rowe Thomas Displays
Designer:	Stuart Stone

This display, one of a number of small truck display properties that travel from location to location, represents one way to exhibit an off-the-road vehicle. The simulated rock, sand, and gravel platform help enhance the function of the vehicle. The sloped angle of the platform aids the audience in viewing the features of the vehicle. A mirror with ragged edges simulated a small pond or puddle while allowing visitors to see the special undercarriage mechanics of this truck.

Exhibitor:	Mayo Clinic Jacksonville
Producer:	Giltspur Exhibits, Boston
Designer:	Malcolm Grear Designers

Light is used to dramatize the story here. The main entrance is dark, with back-lit transparencies, symbolizing the early pioneering years. The visitor travels through this space while experiencing a gradual journey of dark to light, until reaching the main body of the exhibit, which displays the contemporary Mayo Clinic and its prospects for the future.

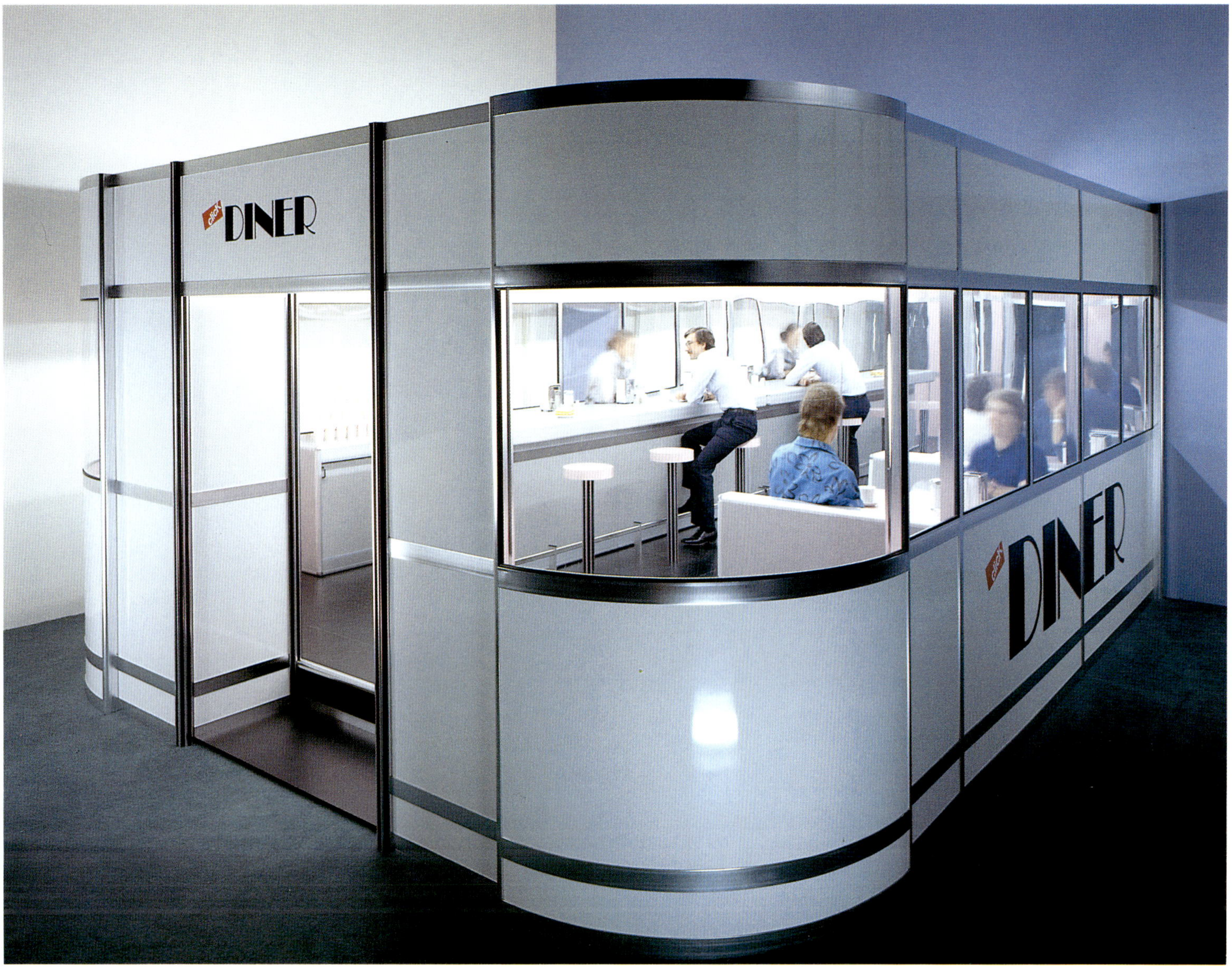

Exhibitor/Producer: Click Systems Ltd.
Designer: Robin Drake

Highly evocative shapes and skillful use of color, finish, and detail make this an outstanding demonstration of the techniques possible with the system.

Exhibitor: AT&T; McDonald's Corp.; Illinois Bell
Producer: Kevmar Exhibits
Designer: Plumb Design Group

To demonstrate the use of a live network of telecommunications at an industry symposium, this exhibit portrayed three locations—headquarters, a regional office and an individual restaurant—to show video conferencing, polling, and training, in a realistic setting.

SOME INTERESTING IDEAS

Exhibitor: Coca Cola USA
Producer: C. Henning Studios Inc.
Designer: Cassandra Henning

The 12-foot rotating globe uses aluminum struts for the framework, lexan panels for the globe, and painted lexan panels for the continents. The row of cups circling the globe rotates in the opposite direction. The support structure is removable so the glove can be used as an independent piece.

Exhibitor: Anheuser-Busch Inc.
Producer/Designer: Heritage Communications of St. Louis Inc.

A portable, easy-to-set-up, table-top exhibit designed for use by distributors to promote alcohol awareness programs. The main limitation was dealing with a relatively large amount of copy and graphic elements, and still create an esthetically pleasing display.

SOME INTERESTING IDEAS 251

Exhibitor: Coca Cola USA
Producer: C. Henning Studios Inc.
Designer: Cassandra Henning

These are two of six tapestries created to define international exhibit areas in an authentic manner, but from an American perspective. Each of the six tapestries was approximately 30-feet tall and 75-feet wide. Due to the size and limited installation time, each tapestry was constructed in a minimal number of sections, transported to the site, and suspended from the beams of the facility.

Exhibitor: Fairview Hall
Producer: Geron Assoc Ltd.
Designer: Ramon Brioux

This 36-foot high castle was developed for a large department store. The elves in the upper section are animated.

SOME INTERESTING IDEAS

INDEX

EXHIBITORS

ADC Telecommunications 63
AGFA Gevaert 155
AT & T 123, 169, 245, 249
AT&T Network Systems 121, 202, 203
Abbott Laboratories 124, 175
Acro Extrusion Company 168
American Electric 184
American Heart Association 68
American Optical 48
American Wood Council 64
Amtrol 162
Analogic 53
Anchor Food Service 186
Anchorage Museum 216
Anheuser-Busch, Inc. 40, 251
Apt Display 50
Astra Pharmaceutical 79
Atlantic Aviation 111
BWD Automotive 160
Bard Cardiosurgery 74
Beecham Products 54
Beef Industry Council 41
Bell Bagg 35
Bell South Services 48
Bissell 91
Black & Decker (U.S.) Inc. 142
Block Island Historical Society 217
Braun 192
British Airways 148
Bunge Corp. 67
Burroughs-Wellcome Co. 76
Bytheway's Mfg. Co. 149
Camex 102
Campbell's 154
Canadair 185
Cardiac Pacemaker, Inc. 152
Cardio Data Systems 55
Carter Press Museum 231
Case Communications 85
Caterpillar 140
Champion International Corp. 51
Champion Spark Plug 164
CheckRobot 157
Christ Science Pub. 228
Clark Equipment Co. 89
Classic Optical 65
CLD-9 38
Click Systems, Inc. 249
Coast to Coast Hardware 244
Coca Cola Foods 204, 205
Coca-Cola USA 98, 132, 133, 250, 252
Colonial Williamsburg 218
Compugraphic Corp. 156
Con Edison 245
Conoco, Inc. 226
Corning Glass 65
Crissa Corp. 88
Crown American 116
Dallas Corp. 105
DePuy, Inc. 84
Dennison National 90

DeWitt Wallace 218
Digital Communications Association 109
Digital Equipment 103
Digital Research, Inc. 56
Digital Technology 34
Display Systems Group 186
Donohoe O'Brien and Associates, Inc. 72
Dr. Pepper 98
Du Pont/Fibers Division 43
Du Pont/PermaSep Products 158
Du Pont/Corian 85
Du Pont 159
Eastman Kodak Co. 60
Edison/Cooper Lighting Group 189
Electrocom Automation 247
Emhart 180
Empire Pencil Corp 61
Equities Prop & Dev 92
Essex 42
Fairchild Industries 242,243
Fairview Hall 253
Father Flanagan's Boy's Town 214, 215
First Tennessee Bank 219
Ford Motor Co 248
Four Seasons Hotel 162, 163
GMC Truck 128, 129
GTE 206, 207
Georgia Institute of Tech 212, 213
Gates Engineering 38
General Data Comm. 71
General Foods 178
German Marshall Fund of U.S. 226
Glaxo Inc. 75
Goodman Segar Hogan 93
Gorman Rupp Co. 151
Gulpen Beer Brewery 66
Halliburton Cos 135
Hamilton Beach Inc. 181
Harcourt Brace Jovanovich 100
Harris Corporation 179
Hazel/Cardinal 238
Herlitz Inc. 78
Hill Refrigeration 106
Hills Bros. Coffee Co. 56, 57
Hilti Inc. 169
Hilton Hotel Corp. 183
Hoechst Chemicals 95
Hoechst-Roussel 70
Honda 140
Honeywell/Test Mgmts. 80
Horton, TL Design 200, 201
Hubbell Steel Co. 51
Huebsch Originators 149
Illinois Bell 249
IBM 52
ICI Americas Inc. 70
IEEE 66
JVC 239
Jaguar 107
Jetway Systems 39
Johnson & Johnson 94
Keller Mfg. 55
Klockner Pentapast 105
Knouse Foods 164
Kohler 197

Konica Med. Corp. 87
L/M Animal Farms 40
Lake County Museum 230
Lasag Int'l. 166
Lederle Labs 165
Libbey St. Clair 193
M/V City of St. Louis 227
Manville/Holophane Div. 47
Master Lock/Dexter 180
Maxwell 184
Mayo Clinic 248
McDonald's Corp. 249
Medical Incorporated 79
Metro-North Commuter Railroad 246
Miles Pharmaceutical 187
Millipore Corp. 144
Minners Designs 57
Mitsubishi 131
Mobil 190
Molex Inc. 63
Monticello Visitor Center 229
NY Public Library 229
NCNB National Bank 209
NGN & Co./Rush 37
NYNEX Corp. 238
National Olympic Committee/Sofi 867
NeoRx 163
Novatel 49
Olin Hunt 172
Olympic/Lucite 191
Oster 178
Owens/Corning Fibers 134
Pacific Bell 110
Pacific Science Center 220, 221
Pellon Corp. 108
Pennzoil, Gumout Division 46
Pentax 104
Pfanstiehl Corp. 170, 171
Pfizer Pigments 62
Pictel Corp. 164
Pier 1 Imports 161
Pierce Foods 73
Pioneer Communications 84
Pratt & Lambert 77
RLI Insurance Co. 49
Rampart Packaging 153
Revere Ware 99
Reynolds & Reynolds 188
Ricoh Corp. 86
Robert Bosch Power Tools 195
Rowenta 174
Royal Doulton 68
Samuel Goldwyn 96
Sandoz Pharmaceuticals 243, 95
Sanitaire 62
Schwinn Bicycle Co. 102
Science Museum of Charlotte 231
Scitex America Corp. 188
Searle Pharmaceutical 223
Silicon Valley Group 173
Smead Mfg. 81
Software Design & Mgmt. 69
Southern Bell 209, 233, 236, 237
Southern Co. 54
Souvenir 37

St. Louis Science Center 222
Star Micronics Inc. 101
Sterling Plastics 156
Sweats/Fizz Ed. 71
Tempo 73
Texaco USA 194
Texas & SW Cattle Raisers 232
Thomson CGR 145
Travenol 150
US Air 246
US West Direct 34
US West Inc. 41, 136, 137, 138, 139
Uniforms To You 89
Union Bank 43
United Longchamp 44, 45
Upjohn Co. Inc. 104
Vail Associates 208
Victor Computer 192
Vistakon 53
Volkswagen USA 130
Vulcan 60
Waste Management Inc. 224, 225
Wetrock Cleaning Supply 108
Wisconsin Electric Power 205
World Book 74
Xerox Corp. 240, 241
YKK Zippers Inc. 97

DESIGNERS

Adell, Shelton 239
Adex Inc. 65, 70
Albitz, Robert 202, 203
Applebaum, Ralph, Assoc. 229
Apt Display 50
Barrett, John 76, 95
Bartle, Jeff 131
Bennett, Bill 84
Bianchi, Dan 39
Bluepeter 110
Bonomi, Cindie 46
Boyce, Mike 78
Brandt, Peter 163, 171, 194
Brioux, Ramon 49, 154, 253
Bryan, Gayle 173
Burk, Dan 88
Burke, Jeff 104, 156, 160
Burke, Timothy Maritz 230
Cash, Kathryn A/Marit 244, 245
Chamberland, Scott 231
Chiaradia, Oscar, Stu 66, 95, 108
Ciaraldi, Paul 193
Ciulla, Vincent, Des 216, 217, 218, 219
Clark, Dottie 79
Connor, Jim 92, 114, 115
Convention Exhibits 67
Corbus, Jane 103
Cournoyer, Jon 222
Couture, Alain 88
Cunitz, John 62
Custom Exhibits 169
Daniel Quan Design 220, 221

Day, Skip 156, 157, 188
DeCarolis, Philip 155
DeMartin, Morona eta 232
Derse Company, The 126, 170
Design & Production, Inc. 231
Design Plus Two 85, 179
Design South 48
Diedrich, David 188
Disney Imagineering 140, 141
Down, George L. 55
Downing Displays 40, 35, 246
Drake, Robin 249
EAS Exhib. Service 185
Echinger, Barry 231
Ehman, Wayne 246
Eisterhold, Gerard 214, 215
Eosbenner, Michael 175
Exhibitgroup/Las Vegas 239
Exhibits Int'l. 68
Expoglass Sistemas 60
Fallen, Ann Catherine 226
Ferguson, Ron 166
Fornes, Jeanne 36
Froom, Charles 229
GOOD SHOW! Inc. 34, 41, 52, 136, 137, 138, 139
Gambrel, Robert 78
Garber, G. 121
Giffin, Dick 152, 238
Gilbert, Mitch 197
Goltry, Kirk 51, 49
Graphic Displays 57
Grear, Malcolm, Des. 248
Groenier, Paul 222
Gronenfeld, Rick 668, 161
Gunderson, Jon 162, 163
Hartwig Exhibitions 62, 149, 180, 181, 189
Hassa, Richard 184
Healey, Dennis 144
Heery & Heery Arch. 213
Heintzelman, Earl 207
Hennessy, Joe 40, 165, 169
Henning, Cassandra 98, 132, 133, 250, 252
Heritage Comm./SL 251
Hilti 169
Hoffman-Dana, Neal 178
Holker, Ralph 165
Holloway, Lynn 209
Horton, Tony 92, 93, 116-117, 120, 117-119, 200-201
Impact Exhibits 60, 86, 123, 124, 125
Inform GmbH 192
Jamison, Kenneth 91
Johnson, Darold 81
Johnson, Doug 140, 130
Johnson, George P., Co. 140-141
Jones, Kent 238
Karpilov, Alex 107, 245
Kelley, Jim 48
King, Stuart 180
Kitzing, Fred 63, 77, 102
Klimov, Alex 202-203
Kolesnik, Chris 51
Konke, Ken 35, 37, 66, 73, 98, 105, 135, 247
LaMotte, Les 56
Laliberte, Jacques 150

Langley, Dorothea 54, 100
Langston, David 97
Lewis, Rick 79, 87, 128-129, 178
Mass, Robert D. 158
MacAllister, Thomas 190
Maher, Paul 222
Malas, David 74
Maricich, Joe 64, 191
Maritz Comm. 205, 224-225
Maritz Dim. Comm. 230
Masters, Jeff 145
Matas, David 74
Matrix Design Cons 43
McDonnell, Brendan 96
McGarry, Robert 62
McKeon, John 246
McMillan, Charles 75, 94
McMillan, Charles/Nancy 226, 228
McVey, Allan 127
Mellow, II, Emil A. 70
Mon, Paul 187
Monger, Barney 130
Morris, Cheri 72
Nardelli, Isabelle 242-243
Nave, Frank D. 175
Nimlok Co. 148
Norenberg, Mark 101, 240-241
Occhipinti, Paul 102, 157
Orr, Michael 66
Orubeondo, Armando 39, 41
PGAV Design, Inc. 227
Pafk, Tom 36
Panzarella, Joseph 99
Pentes, Jack 209
Petty, Guy 163
Pingel Displays Inc. 55
Plan 3 67, 192
Plumb Design Group 43, 121, 249
Rafla, Jeffrey 205
Randall, Lee 148
Raustiala, George 90
Reynolds, Tony 64, 191
Riday, Rick 64
Riggio, Barbara A. 38, 105, 168
Rios, Roger M. 47, 80, 208
Roberts, Gina 184
Rothan, Matt 64
Rumsey, Richard 53
Russell, Al 84
Ryan, Teddi Jo 153
S. Laird Jenkins Corp. 73
Schneider, Jack 63
Showalter, Dean 102
Smith, Henry 72
Smith, Tim 92
Sosa, Jorge O. 245
Spicuzza, Martin 42, 74, 143, 151, 184, 196
Stone, Stuart 89, 248
Stough, George W. 236-237, 209, 233
Sugar Creek Studios 54, 71, 74, 108, 109, 195, 212-213, 223
Svetlik, Fred 53, 89, 164
TGA Displays, Inc. 56-57
Thompson, Ross 77
360 Designers & Producers 149

INDEX

Ting, Roger 172, 243
Tucker, Bill 84
United Longchamp Int'l. 44-45, 106, 244
Utrecht, Karl 104
Van Sickle & Rolleri 43, 85, 111, 159
Viamonte, Joe 187
Visual Fabrications 37, 71
Watkins, Raymond 61
Weitzman, Mark 134
Wendel, Chris 130
Wilen, John 174, 186
Wittler, Waldemar 122
Woerdehoff, Klaus 69
Wollen, Craig 191
Yurkin, Tom 183

PRODUCERS

360 Designers & Prod. 149
Adex Inc. 65, 70
Admore Inc. 94
Adv. Display & Exh. 222
All West Display 64, 191
Art Guild Inc. 43, 111, 85, 159
Artley 43
Ausstell, K1 Woerdeh 69
Bluepeter 110
Boss Display Corp. 84
Brace, David Displays 36, 53
Chamberland, Scott 231
Chiaradia, Oscar, Stu 66, 95, 108
Click Systems, Inc. 65, 231, 249
Color & Design 216
Condit Exhibits 52
Convention Exhibits 67
Crampton Inc. 104
Custom Exhibits Corp. 169
Custom Fix Displays 204-205
Cyclonics, Inc. 42, 74, 1420143, 151, 196, 166
Denby Associates 238
Derse Co. 126, 127, 170, 205
Design & Production 218
Design Agency, The 150
Design Craftsmen 104, 224-225
Design Dynamics/Exh 47, 80, 208
Design Realizations 55
Design South 48
Dimensional Des. & Dec. 173
Dimension Works 53, 89, 174, 164, 186
Dinamation of California 220
Display Arts Studios 38, 70, 105, 158, 168
Display Service Co. 187
Display Workshop 157, 188
Downing Displays 40, 34, 246
ECOFA 165
Eisterhold Lewellyn 214-215
Euro Domestic Exhib 230
Exhibit Co., The 48
Exhibit Des Cons 64, 191
Exhibit Source Inc. 49, 51
Exhibit by Design 104, 156, 160
Exhibit Group/Chicago 79, 87, 127, 128-129, 166, 178
Exhibit Group/Cincinnati 188, 206-207
Exhibit Group/Las Vegas 239
Exhibit Group/New York 90, 107, 184, 229, 232, 245
Exhibit Group/San Francisco 38, 39, 40
Exhibits Inc. 34, 41, 136-137, 138-139, 178
Exhibits Int'l. 68, 193
ExpoSystems 73
Expoglass Sistemas Modulares 60
Exponents, Inc. 91, 140-141, 194
Fahey Exhibits 102, 145, 144, 157
Freeman Design Disp. 68, 161, 163, 183
Gallo Displays 84
Geron Assoc. Ltd. 49, 154, 180, 253
Giltspur/Boston 51, 76, 95, 103, 122, 248
Giltspur/Chicago 163, 194
Giltspur/Pittsburgh 46, 54, 79, 100, 130, 242-243
Giltspur/Rochester 101, 190, 240-241
Government of India 221
Graphic Displays 57
Guest, RH, Inc. 217
Haas Display 81, 152, 238
Hartwig Exhibitions 62, 149, 180, 181, 189
Henning Studios Inc. 98, 132-133, 250, 252
Heritage Comm/St. Louis 40, 164, 169, 227, 251
Heritage Display/Dallas 35, 37, 66, 73, 98, 105, 134, 135, 197, 247
Heritage Display/St. Paul 63, 148
Horton, T L, Design 72, 92, 93, 114-115, 116-117, 117-119, 120, 200-201
Impact Exhibits, Inc. 60, 86, 124, 125, 123, 175
Inform GmbH 192
Innovations Inc. 74
Intro Displays 172, 243
Johnson, Geo P., Co. 131, 140-141, 202-203
Kadoke Display 185
Kevmar 121, 249
Kitzing, Inc. 63, 77, 99, 102
Las Vegas Conv Prod 162
Maltbie, Charles, Assoc. 187, 229
Mancini, David C. 219
Matrix Exhibits 61, 96
McCormick Display 88
McMillan Gp 226
McMillan Gp/Scotia 228
Midwest/Backer 222
Moss Exhibits 50
Murphy & Orr Co. 209, 233, 236-237
Nimlock Co. 148
Pacific Sci Center 220, 221
Pentes Design 209
Pingel Displays Inc. 55
Plan 3 69, 192
PML Exhibit Services Ltd. 216
PR Guest, Inc. 217
Presentations South 62
Production House 85, 179
Research & Des Assoc. 226
Robinson, W. Scott, Designs 220
Rowe Thomas Displays 89, 248
Sci Mus of Charlotte 231
Skyline Displays 39, 56, 78
Structural Display 155
Sugar Creek Studios 54, 71, 75, 97, 109, 108, 195, 212-213, 223
Superior Phototech 217
Syma Systems Inc. 246
TGA Displays, Inc. 56-57
United Longchamp Int'l. 44-45, 106, 244
Universal Exhibits 42
Visual Fabrications 37, 71